Oak Park Historic
Preservation
Commission

Village of Oak Park,
Oak Park, Illinois

1999

Managing Editor
Molly Wickes
Associate Editor
Kate Irvin
Design studio blue

**A Guide
to Oak Park's**

Frank Lloyd Wright

**and Prairie
School Historic
District**

Contents

Preface and acknowledgments

In 1973 the Frank Lloyd Wright-Prairie School of Architecture Historic District was placed on the National Register of Historic Places, a federally managed list of historically and culturally significant properties. The district is loosely defined by the boundaries of Division Street on the north, Lake Street on the south, Ridgeland Avenue on the east, and Marion Street on the west. With twenty-six structures designed by Frank Lloyd Wright, America's most famous architect, and over sixty buildings designed by members of the Prairie School, this approximately one-square-mile area has the highest concentration of Prairie-style houses in the world.

While internationally famous as the birthplace of the Prairie style, Oak Park is less well known for its other types of well-preserved architecture, ranging from the simple farmhouses of its early settlers to the huge estates of Chicago's industrial giants. In addition to their architectural significance, these structures also provide a context for understanding the work of the Prairie School. Taken as a whole, the district encapsulates the major trends in residential architecture of the late nineteenth and early twentieth centuries and illuminates Oak Park's growth and development as a community.

Although this guidebook contains information on 118 structures, not every building of architectural and historical interest could be included. Far from attempting to offer the definitive word on the district's holdings, we hope that this book encourages additional study and provides a basis for further exploration not only of Oak Park but also of other historic neighborhoods in America.

The first guidebook to the Frank Lloyd Wright-Prairie School of Architecture Historic District was published in 1976 as a result of the efforts of the Oak Park Landmarks Commission and the Oak Park Bicentennial Commission of the American Revolution. Written by architectural historian Paul Sprague, *Guide to the Frank Lloyd Wright and Prairie School Architecture in Oak Park* was an immediate success, and in 1986 a fourth edition was published. Through Sprague's guidebook, visitors and residents alike have gained a deeper understanding of the work of the Prairie School. Increasingly, however, people have begun to recognize that Oak Park's architectural heritage consists of more than Frank Lloyd Wright-designed homes. In 1992 the Oak Park Historic Preservation Commission initiated plans to publish a comprehensive guidebook to the district, which, in addition to updating the material on its Prairie-style buildings, would also include information on other architecturally and historically significant structures.

The commission is greatly indebted to the volunteer efforts of Oak Park residents Lesley Gilmore, Carol Kelm, David Sokol, Lin Von Dreele, and Peg Zak, each of whom is responsible for one of the tours in the guidebook. Noted architectural photographers Patrick Linehan, Jamie Padgett, Kate Roth, Leslie Schwartz, and Bruce Van Inwegen provided the photographs. Alice Sinkevitch contributed the introduction. Additionally, many thanks must go to Molly Wickes, the managing editor, whose perseverance and expertise brought this project to completion.

Finally, the Commission would like to thank the Village of Oak Park and its trustees, whose continuous support made the publishing and distribution of this book possible.

Dennis Langley
Chair, Guidebook Committee
Oak Park Historic
Preservation Commission

Introduction

An independent spirit has long been cited as an American, and especially a Midwestern, characteristic. Chicago's sturdy and felicitous suburb of Oak Park is living proof. Not coincidentally, Oak Park's formative years were the years of residence of that persuasive visionary Frank Lloyd Wright. Rapid growth and a strong sense of place made Oak Park the perfect spot for a young architect to rethink and create anew the American home.

In the late-nineteenth century, "independent" was not to be confused with "radical." Throughout the country, and especially in industrial cities such as Chicago, there was a great fear of radicalism, which was inextricably linked with labor unrest. In 1898 William Halley wrote in *Pictorial Oak Park*:

"We have not developed any marked peculiarity in the way of municipal methods, mentality, politics or religion. No one has distinguished our town by being the especial apostle of any particular species of doctrine or ethics. We have given to the world no hero, no great genius; we have cultivated no species. Our only claim is that by purpose and perseverance we have built up a beautiful town that is possessed of every home advantage."

But dedication to the "home advantage" and to independent thought made for a conservative community that respected and nurtured innovation. Within five years of the publication of *Pictorial Oak Park*, Ernest Hemingway was born, Frank Lloyd Wright created the first Prairie-style houses, and community leaders devised creative legislation that enabled Chicago's suburbs to avoid annexation to the city.

Chicago grew only half as far west as it did north and south. The city's cinched shape is due to the perseverance and legislative innovations of the leaders of late-nineteenth-century Oak Park. Chicago climbed from 44 to 170 square miles through the annexations of 1889, leaving the city's western boundary a mere 1.5 miles east of what became Oak Park's eastern boundary, Austin Boulevard. As a village within Cicero Township, Oak Parkers had chafed under taxation without representation for forty years. The battle for freedom from the township and safety from annexation was waged in the courts, the polling places, and the state legislature throughout the 1890s.

After an 1899 township vote that subjected rival Austin to annexation by Chicago, it was determined that there were no legal means of creating a separate village of Oak Park from the old township. Local leaders won from the Illinois General Assembly in 1901 passage of a bill that made their independence legal and gave other Illinois communities the mechanism to do the same.

Oak Park had grown slowly until the start of rail service west from Chicago in 1848. Real-estate developers and early landowners subdivided the prairie and farms in the 1850s and 1860s, but the devastating Chicago Fire of 1871 led many more to seek homes in the suburbs. Oak Park's population grew from 500 in 1870 to 4,500 in 1890 and quadrupled in the next twenty years. Creating the homes and the churches, the schools and the stores that families needed was big business.

Frank Lloyd Wright arrived in this rapidly growing community in the late 1880s. He was much like his neighbors and clients, a young man with a family, making his way in the world not with inherited wealth but on the basis of his skills and wits. He lived in Oak Park until 1909 and during these years developed the personal vision that changed architecture, first in Oak Park, and then around the world. The interest his neighbors and clients had in their homes and their design gave him the arena in which to become, as he later said, "the world's greatest architect."

Oak Park can serve as a textbook of the styles of American homes from the 1870s to the 1930s: Gothic Revival, Italianate, Stick, Queen Anne, Shingle, Prairie, the popular post-World War I revivals, and Art Moderne. Elements of these styles flavor even the smallest houses and dignify most apartment buildings. Under the shelter of the rich canopy of Oak Park trees, they dazzlingly complement and contrast with each other and exalt the routines of everyday life.

Alice Sinkevitch
Hon. AIA
Executive Director of the American
Institute of Architects
Chicago Chapter

How to use the guidebook

Every building is numbered, named (in most cases the first owner of the house), and listed with the address, architect, and construction date. For those entries whose significance is based on a historic remodeling, that date is provided as well; other remodeling dates are not included. Because of the large number of buildings within the guidebook, not every building could be photographed.

Each structure is identified by style. Though learning to recognize styles can be rewarding, these labels should be used as a general guide only. The great wealth and variety of Oak Park's Prairie-style and Prairie-style-influenced architecture, in particular, makes this task difficult. Within the guidebook, Prairie style has been broadly defined to include not only the work of Frank Lloyd Wright and his followers but also much of the work of George Maher and E. E. Roberts, whose versions of the Prairie style were quite different from Frank Lloyd Wright's. While we have used broad stylistic categories in American architecture whenever possible, there are a few exceptions: the term "pre-Prairie" has been applied to a few early Frank Lloyd Wright homes that predicted the development of his full-fledged Prairie style; and "Eclectic" has been applied to houses that feature elements from many different styles in such a way that no one style dominates. Since the identifying features of a style, its occurrence, period of popularity, and even name can vary regionally, a style guide has been included on page 136.

tour

a

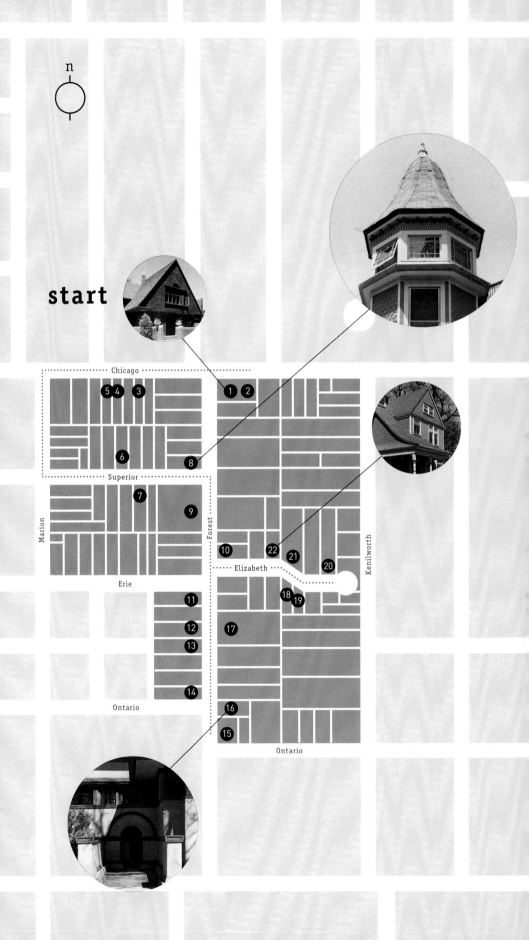

start

Chicago

5 4 3

1 2

6

8

Superior

7

9

Marion

Forest

10

22

21

20

Kenilworth

Elizabeth

18

19

11

17

12

13

Erie

14

Ontario

16

15

Ontario

This tour comprises the greatest concentration of Frank Lloyd Wright's buildings in the historic district, covering fifteen of his twenty-eight Oak Park structures. These examples – whether additions, remodelings, or new homes – represent a broad range of Wright's ideas and talents over a considerable span of time (1889 to 1923) and demonstrate Wright's evolution from a fledgling apprentice into a mature architect. The district also offers a full spectrum of housing development and architectural design in Oak Park, much of which preceded Wright's residence and practice in Oak Park and exemplifies the ideas from which Wright dissented.

The late-nineteenth-century Italianate and Queen Anne homes were typically composed of the boxy, divided rooms that Wright tried to dissolve. Over several years Wright transformed his home **1** from a Victorian Shingle-style building with a traditional floor plan into an inventive and open connection of spaces for living and working. These changes provide tangible evidence of Wright's struggle and success at realizing his intellectual goals in built form. The modifications to the home and studio reveal the young architect's growth as a person and his need to break from what he perceived as restraint.

During the early 1900s, Frank Lloyd Wright's contemporaries also began to design in the Prairie style, as seen in E. E. Roberts's own house at 1019 Superior Street **7** . The growing popularity of the Prairie style is also reflected in the many houses that were remodeled around this time. The Italianate home at 223 North Forest **12** that was transformed into a Prairie-style house in 1906 is a robust representative of the widespread support of the Prairie School in Oak Park. Stucco was the vinyl siding of the 1910s and 1920s, with far greater physical and aesthetic impact.

This tour begins at the start of Wright's career with his own house of 1889 and his bootleg houses of 1892–93 on Chicago Avenue. Forest Avenue reveals a strong mix of architecturally significant Victorian homes alongside the Wright-designed Prairie-style houses that alternately shocked and pleased those who first saw them. The side trip down the curved Elizabeth Court is only one block long and features some of the earlier homes in the area and their individual stylistic transformations.

tour

a

Tour A is approximately 1 mile

Estimated walking time 70 minutes

428 North Forest
Frank Lloyd Wright
Shingle style
1889–1895

951 Chicago
Frank Lloyd Wright
Prairie style
1898

Frank Lloyd Wright Home and Studio ❶, ❷ Wright and his mother purchased this corner site in 1889. His mother paid for her portion with proceeds from the sale of her house in Madison, Wisconsin, and Wright's share was advanced to him by his employer, Louis Sullivan. The same year, at age twenty-two, Wright married Catherine Tobin and soon after built his first home on the southwest portion of the lot. Wright's mother established her home 28 in the existing Gothic Revival cottage at the east end of the site. The west portion remained overgrown, providing a ripe palette for Wright to establish himself as a residential architect by building his home and studio there in 1889 and 1898, respectively. He continued over the years to transform the property and experiment with design concepts.

The modified Shingle-style home has smooth shingled surfaces and an asymmetrical plan. Wright chose a building style that was easily accepted by his neighbors, but that also allowed him to make a distinct statement early in his career. The expansive, dominant roof protects the first floor, compressing the building and surrounding it with wide eaves. Wright made an upstairs bedroom his work space, in addition to his office in downtown Chicago, until he completed the adjacent studio in 1898. In 1895 he reconfigured and enlarged his house, building an addition with a kitchen on the first floor and a kindergarten on the second, and transforming the original kitchen into a dining room. The barrel-vaulted playroom was a unique form that Wright used only a few times in his career. This successful child-scaled room was used by Catherine for classes in which she introduced the neighborhood children to Froebel blocks.

In contrast to the home, the forms and massing of the studio mark a significant departure from the residential structures to which Oak Parkers were accustomed. Wright maintained a residential scale, but created a design that distinguished between the residential and commercial functions of the two buildings. The octagonal geometric shapes, imperceptible roofs, penetrating masses, and window arrangements contribute to the uniqueness of the studio's appearance, though Wright softened the distinction by cladding the building with the same materials as his home – brick and shingles.

The central entry block is the most ornamented, formal area in the studio complex. Distanced from the passerby and street by a low brick wall (origi-

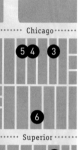

1

2

nally a spindled balustrade), the entry sequence is discovered as it is traversed. Expressive figures crouch atop the entry piers, and the plaster capitals in the entry incorporate abstracted allegorical forms. These elements, designed by sculptor Richard Bock, welcome the visitor to a place in which architecture is clearly considered to be one of the Arts.

The library and the two-story studio space comprise the main work rooms of the studio building. Wright designed the library for optimal storage and display; built-in cabinetry defines the perimeter, and clerestory windows above provide natural light. Inside Wright used materials – sand-float plaster with a glazed finish, magnesite flooring (creating a feeling of warmth in the reception room), and clear-finished wood banding – that are similar in texture and composition to those used in to his residential work. The reception room, a transitional space between the library and studio, is lit from above by gold and green art glass that gives the impression of a canopy of trees. These rectangular art-glass panels are oriented lengthwise, directing visitors east to the drafting room. Compared to the entry, the interior of the relatively large, square drafting room with balcony and pyramidal roof expresses a much different geometry. Chains suspended from the exposed roof framing support a balcony. This inventive structural treatment allows the two-story space to be column-free; the large expanse of glass in the walls of the upper octagonal story emphasizes the roof's soaring, uninterrupted journey. The horizontal thrust of the roofing is countered by a tension ring of linked horizontal chains, thus eliminating the need for cross-bracing, which would effectively weigh the roof down. In 1911 Wright removed the vertical portions of this clever device when he remodeled the balcony level into bedrooms for his family. The lower portion of the drafting room became the living room, and the house was rented out.

Wright last lived in the house in 1909. He left in September of that year and traveled with Mamah Cheney to Berlin, where he worked on the Wasmuth portfolio drawings.

He sold the property in 1925, and it remained in private hands until its purchase was initiated in 1974 by the Frank Lloyd Wright Home and Studio Foundation. In 1975 the National Trust for Historic Preservation became a costeward. The grass-roots campaign to acquire the property represented the combined efforts of the Oak Park Development Corporation, local banks, and concerned citizens. The Trust owns the buildings and the Foundation manages them; they have restored both structures to their 1909 appearance. The property was designated a National Historic Landmark in 1976 and an Oak Park landmark in 1996.

1019
Chicago

Frank Lloyd
Wright

Queen Anne

1892

3

Robert P. Parker House ③   When Thomas Hart Gale commissioned this house, and the nearly identical one at 1027 Chicago Avenue ④ , Frank Lloyd Wright was still working in Adler and Sullivan's office. He was supplementing his income by "moonlighting" – designing buildings after regular working hours for his own clients. The plans of these two houses mirror that of Wright's 1892 Robert Emmond House in La Grange, Illinois. All three houses have the asymmetrical massing, steeply pitched roofs, and interior layouts typical of the Queen Anne style. Wright, however, was already breaking the mold by deviating from the style in profound ways. The characteristic vertical emphasis of the Queen Anne style is present in the two-story bay, yet it is strongly contrasted by the connected bands of windows in the bay and the one-story mass dominated by the adjacent main hipped roof. The walls are clad with only one material, clapboard, rather than a variety of materials as is common to the style. Also lacking are the spindlework and the classical components commonly featured on contemporaneous Queen Anne homes. These bootleg homes point in the direction Wright would take in the 1893 Woolley House ⑥ and subsequent designs.

1027
Chicago
Frank Lloyd
Wright
Queen Anne
1892

4

Thomas H. Gale House ④   Thomas Hart Gale commissioned this house, as well as the one at 1019 Chicago Avenue ③ , from Frank Lloyd Wright in 1892. Gale sold the latter house to Robert Parker before construction was completed. He resided here with his wife, Laura, and two children. In both homes the entry and the side porches were not built as originally designed. The porches, as Wright conceived them, were not typical of their decorative and vertically oriented Queen Anne-style counterparts. His plans called for a low clapboard wall, now reconstructed in the Robert Parker House, that would give the building a horizontal emphasis. The interiors of both homes were composed in Queen Anne fashion, including a formal entry hall and stairway, separate servants' stairs, and well-defined rooms for reception, reading (library), and dining, each divided by pocket doors. The Gales moved to a new home in Oak Park in 1898. After Thomas Gale died in 1907, his widow moved to a house designed by Wright at 6 Elizabeth Court ⑱ .

Walter H. Gale House    The Walter H. Gale House is one of the first buildings Frank Lloyd Wright designed after he broke his five-year contract with the architectural firm of Adler and Sullivan and opened his own office in 1893. The interplay of varied masses and the Palladian window in the side gable evoke the Queen Anne style. However, early expressions of Wright's individualistic style emerge in the continuous band of second-floor windows on the round tower, the tall, narrow dormer, the entrance moved to the side, and the open entry porch with plain spindlework. As in the Thomas Gale and Robert Parker houses (4 and 3), the primary roof steeply descends to the first floor creating a strong horizontal line at the eaves. Walter Gale, an older brother of Thomas H. Gale, operated the retail drugstore established by his father, Edwin O. Gale, an Oak Park pioneer. Walter was one of the first three graduates of the Oak Park and River Forest High School.

**1031
Chicago**

**Frank Lloyd
Wright**

Queen Anne

1893

Francis J. Woolley House 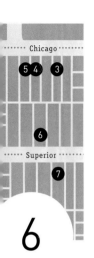 6   The design of this simple residence hints at Wright's later stylistic direction. It reflects the plan and massing of the Robert Parker and Thomas Gale houses (3 and 4), which preceded it by one year, save for the hipped roof that caps the entire building. In those earlier houses, the full-height corner bays read as towers; in the Woolley House, the roof terminates them. Wright's use of a hipped roof signifies a departure from the standard front gable present on most Queen Annes. By reducing the height of the building, he made it less imposing, more of-the-earth. The limestone piers rising above the porch floor to support the broad square columns also indicate Wright's transition to the Prairie style, as do the low clapboard-sided knee walls that enclose the porch. According to grandson Frank Woolley, the interior was completely redecorated within five years of construction after the mechanical system malfunctioned. Wright is purported to have made suggestions for the repairs.

6

**1030
Superior**

**Frank Lloyd
Wright**

Queen Anne

1893

1019
Superior

E. E.
Roberts

Prairie style

remodeling
1911

7

Eben Ezra Roberts House ⑦ Architect E. E. Roberts moved into this house in 1896, three years after his arrival in Oak Park. In 1911, when Roberts remodeled the original house, he doubled the width, added the projecting entrance bay, and coated the house with stucco (changes documented by Sanborn Fire Insurance maps). At the same time, he reconfigured the windows, cantilevered a flat roof over the entry, and built the brick wall in front of the entry. Like many of the houses he designed in the Prairie idiom, Roberts presented the walls as solid planar elements with punched openings. He rarely utilized the Prairie convention of horizontal wood banding to connect the exterior components, as Wright did. The interior of Roberts's home, however, is more characteristically Prairie in the treatment of spaces and in the continuation of the wood trim and detailing inside. Roberts is purported to have designed more than 200 buildings in Oak Park. His popularity helped further the progress and acceptance of Prairie School architecture.

401 North
Forest
Frank Ellis
Queen Anne
1890

8

Sampson and Clara Rogers House 8   Sampson and Clara Rogers bought
this property from real-estate developer E. O. Gale in 1884. The original
Queen Anne structure has been modified extensively over the years. The
multisided porch that envelops the octagonal tower and the second story of
the Forest Avenue porch were added before 1908 and 1915, respectively.
Additionally, in 1912 the second owners, Horatio and Marion Norton, invest-
ed $4,000 to convert the house into two apartments. Though somewhat
obscured by these additions and those at the rear of the building, several
features of the home typify traditional Queen Anne designs: the corner tower, the contrasting cladding materials, and the asymmetrical massing
accented by the full-height bays and subsidiary roofs. The arches that connect the columns on the one-story porch on Forest Avenue, part of the
original design, were elements common to the earlier Italianate style. The
later porch additions, with simple classical detailing and solid massing,
are indicative of the classical revival styles popular when the modifications
were made.

Nathan Grier Moore House ❾ In 1895 attorney Nathan Moore commissioned Wright to design a home in the English style for his family. Wright satisfied his client by presenting him with a substantial half-timbered and brick three-story residence with a steep gabled roof. This building's floor plan and elevations reflect its orientation along the north edge of the property line, which allows for an ample south-facing lawn. The north facade, adjacent to the street, contains an understated entry and several punched openings; and the southern facade, considerably more relaxed, engages the lawn with its broad, open porch.

When the building burned in 1922, Wright designed a new house on the original foundation, making substantial modifications to his preceding design. The 1895 version had three stories, more elaborate half-timbering, and the eaves of the steep roof aligned with the top of the second-floor windows. The 1923 redesign reduced the structure to two stories, with eaves that extended to the top of the first-floor windows. Despite its steep roof, the house has a strong connection to the ground. Wright counterbalanced this emphatic horizontality with pronounced vertical elements, such as the bedroom windows in the two south cross gables, the half-timbering, and the thin, slablike chimneys.

Directly south of the Moore House is the Hills-DeCaro House ㉔, which Wright remodeled for Moore's daughter, Mrs. Edward Hills, in 1906.

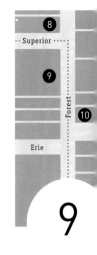

9

333 North Forest

Frank Lloyd Wright

Tudor Revival

1923

300 North
Forest

Architect
unknown

Queen Anne

1893

10

a

Charles Abraham and Anna C. Purcell House ⑩   Built in 1893 for
Charles and Anna Purcell, this large residence illustrates evolving architectural preferences. Sanborn Fire Insurance maps and early photographs trace
changes to the house that reflect the fluctuating tastes of modern times. In
1907 the Purcells moved into a Prairie-style house in River Forest that their
son, architect William Gray Purcell, designed for them. The new owners,
Louis and Narcissa Yager, hired architect Charles E. White to design alterations in 1923. Because the Yagers appreciated the Queen Anne style of their
home, White retained the asymmetrical massing and character of the building while adding classical revival accents. After 1947 new owners replaced
the original half-width front entry porch with a deeper, full-width wraparound porch. Unlike the original porch with spindlework and turned posts,
the new porch is supported by paired square columns with no ornament.
While the size and shape of this porch are not uncommon in Queen Anne
homes, its uninterrupted, simple massing and lack of ornament indicate that
it is a later addition.

231 North
Forest

Architect
unknown

Gothic
Revival/
Italianate

c. 1880s

11

Egbert C. Cook House ⑪   Both Gothic Revival and Italianate influences are evident in this simple vernacular building. Such eclectic mixtures were not uncommon and illustrate the stylistic evolution of the 1880s. The earlier Gothic Revival style, popularized by builders' pattern books following the Civil War, was on the wane, while the slightly later Italianate style continued to be popular in Oak Park into the mid-1880s. The vertical emphasis given to the building by the tall, front-facing gable, the vergeboard (or "ginger-bread") decorating the rakes of both gables, and the open eaves show the influence of the Gothic Revival. The Italianate features – the window trim, and the paired windows in the second story – are more subtle components of the composition. The L-shaped plan and one-story porch inside the "L" were common to both styles. The shutters, classical front porch, and full-height extension at the rear of the building are subsequent modifications. Egbert C. Cook bought this property from Emily and Orlando Blackmer (see ⑭) in 1881 and lived there with his wife and daughter until at least 1897.

Albert H. Vilas House 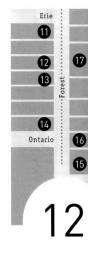 The Prairie-style Vilas house should be carefully compared with the Italianate house immediately to the south of it, for they were once nearly identical buildings. In 1906 contractors Sias and Grenfell transformed the original exterior, creating a hipped-roof, four-square house with overhanging eaves, stucco-clad walls, and broad front porch. Grouped casement windows took the place of the original tall, narrow Italianate windows. In the interior a masculine rectilinear stair with square spindles and square newel posts replaced the sweeping open stair with turned balusters and carved newel posts. Before and after photographs of the house appeared in a local publication in 1907, which advertised the changes as the "S. & G. Treatment." The alterations followed a trend, lasting through the 1920s, in which builders clad Victorian-era homes throughout Oak Park in stucco – a good illustration of the influence of Wright and other Prairie School architects.

223 North Forest

Architect unknown

Italianate/ Prairie style

c.1880s

remodeling 1906

Henderson and Sarah Judd House 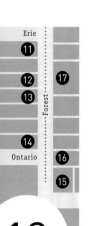 The Judd House contains the identifying features of the Italianate style: low-pitched hipped roof; overhanging eaves supported by scrolled brackets; and tall, narrow windows. The style began in England and was promoted in America by Andrew Jackson Downing's architectural pattern books based on rural Italian farmhouses. It was dominant in the United States between 1850 and 1880 and enjoyed a later run in the Midwest, continuing to appear throughout the 1880s. Few such structures remain in Oak Park today.

The Judd House also reflects changing stylistic preferences in the Midwest. The non-original front porch echoes the classically inspired buildings of the 1893 World's Columbian Exposition in Chicago, which heavily influenced building styles for the next fifty years. Comparison with the Prairie-style stucco home immediately to the north, at 223 North Forest **12**, rounds out the historical picture, for the two houses were once nearly identical.

Sarah and Reverend Henderson Judd bought this property from the Blackmers (see **14**) in 1881 and sold it to Margaret and William Halkett in 1888.

Erie
11
12 **17**
13
Forest
14
Ontario **16**
15

13

219 North Forest

Architect unknown

Italianate

1882

203 North
Forest

Architect
unknown

Queen Anne

1882

14

Orlando and Emily Blackmer House (14)   The Blackmer House has survived numerous threats to its existence throughout the years, including fires of varying impact and a proposed demolition to provide land for a five-story YMCA building. Despite its beleaguered existence, the character of the original house has survived. Its Queen Anne style is expressed in the complex massing, integral second-floor porch, turned posts on the first-floor porch, decorative shingles in all gables, and smooth, curved cornice unifying the second-floor roofs.

Orlando and Emily Blackmer, who in 1881 were actively involved in buying and selling property on this side of the block, sold this house to Amaretta S. and Russell K. Bickford in 1884. Orlando Blackmer was a typical early Oak Park resident. Born in Barnard, Vermont, in 1827, Blackmer graduated from Williams College in 1853 and came west to teach. He formed a publishing firm in Rockford, Illinois, around 1860 and moved to Oak Park in 1866; during these years he relocated the business to Chicago.

200–206
North Forest

William J.
Van Keuren

Queen Anne

1892

15

Emerson Ingalls Row Houses **15**   Masonry Queen Anne structures are generally a rare building type. The Ingalls buildings are among the few such remaining in Oak Park, and they are the only row houses in this historic district. Trademarks of the Queen Anne style include the asymmetry of each unit and the contrasting textures of the smooth, pressed brick and rough-hewn stone. The rugged stone arches and rounded window bays indicate the influence of the Romanesque Revival upon masonry structures in the 1890s. Though the porches have been rebuilt, the two northernmost units retain much of the original detailing. In true Victorian fashion, a limestone curb, with markers for each entry, gently defines the perimeter of the private property.

Austin Gardens is directly opposite, on the west side of the street. This public park was once the grounds of the home built in 1860 by Henry Austin, one of the first settlers of Oak Park. A bronze bust of Frank Lloyd Wright graces the northeast corner of the site.

Frank W. Thomas House **16** The Frank W. Thomas House is Wright's first "Prairie House" in the Chicago area, as well as the first Oak Park house Wright designed with a grade-level basement and raised living spaces. The latter characteristic, combined with the covered terrace, high walls, and recessed entry, contributes to a gentle privacy throughout the L-shaped house. This atmosphere is accentuated by the warm materials and strong horizontal emphasis, creating the illusion of a much smaller building. The exterior stucco finish, horizontal wood banding, and concrete water table were to become hallmarks of Wright's Prairie houses.

The house was commissioned by James Rogers, who gave it to his daughter and son-in-law, Susan and Frank W. Thomas. Rogers built the home on the former site of Grace Episcopal Church, which had relocated to 924 Lake Street by 1898. Tallmadge and Watson designed a large rear addition in 1922 with materials and detailing similar to those in the original house.

16

210 North Forest

Frank Lloyd Wright

Prairie style

1901

238 North
Forest

Frank Lloyd
Wright

Prairie style

remodeling
1906

17

Peter A. Beachy House ⑰   As is typical of Wright's remodeling commissions, here the original nineteenth-century Gothic Revival cottage is not detectable. When viewed from the street, the long gabled roof broken by a regular series of cross gables predominates over the structure. The house looks compact and grounded, with the large veranda acting as a dynamic appendage. Wright's characteristic division of masses is developed here in the facade's dominant lintels, sills, and copings, all of which are counterbalanced by understated vertical posts and cornerboards. The smooth stucco, concrete, and wood contrast with the rough texture of the brick.

Peter Beachy, a wealthy banker, lived in the house through 1942; later owners converted the house into a duplex. After a 1990 fire resulted in extensive fire and water damage, the current owners, with the aid of Wright's drawings, returned the home to the original design configuration.

6 Elizabeth
Frank Lloyd
Wright
Prairie style
1909

18

Mrs. Thomas H. Gale House 18 Frank Lloyd Wright's drawings for this sculpturally dynamic house are dated to 1904, yet construction did not begin until 1909, two years after Thomas Gale's premature death. Thomas's widow, Laura Gale, lived here with her two children until her death in 1943.

The building's varied forms, complex massing, and strong contrast between solid and void – accentuated by the cantilevered balconies – belie the tranquility of the interiors. Simply proportioned and finished rooms provide a calming departure from the exterior. Wright manipulated pedestrian movement outside and inside the home; the side entry, once discovered behind the stucco pier, directs the visitor into the hall behind the living room fireplace, which Wright placed asymmetrically to the built-in cabinetry. Many of the ideas that Wright introduced here were further developed in his 1935 design of Fallingwater, in Pennsylvania, for the Edgar J. Kaufmann, Sr., family.

Reverend Joseph Edwin Roy House  Joseph Roy built this home in the early months of 1871 at the southeast corner of Kenilworth and Erie, in time to view the glow of the Chicago Fire in October of that year. In 1899 the Roys relocated their home to its present site, rotating the building so it would face the new curved street. The home is a substantial rendition of a Gothic Revival cottage, with a steeply pitched roof, thin dormers, pointed windows, and a quatrefoil in the front gable screen. Originally the house had two-over-two sash windows without shutters, and double doors without side-lights marked the entry. The front porch, previously featuring scroll-sawn wood ornaments, now has iron railings and posts.

The local papers described Reverend Roy as "among the last truly large, broad-visioned men espousing an unpopular cause" – he was a leading figure who petitioned the abolition of slavery directly to President Lincoln. The Reverend died at home in 1908 at age 82. His son, Joseph H. Roy, built the Queen Anne residence next door, at 10 Elizabeth Court, circa 1900.

19

8 Elizabeth

Architect unknown

Gothic Revival

1871

Kennedy Coach House  The compelling house at 9 Elizabeth Court was originally constructed as the coach house to the large Queen Anne home, the Kennedy House, at 309 North Kenilworth, directly to the east. The iron fencing at the front of the lot remains from the original fencing for the entire Kennedy property, which also included a windmill and pump adjacent to the coach house. Sub-division of the property made both buildings more affordable.

A $6,900 conversion by Mr. and Mrs. C. R. Boynton in 1940 transformed the coach house into a single-family home. The carriage room and stalls of the first floor were turned into the kitchen, living room, and dining alcove, and the coachman's quarters upstairs became bedrooms. Set far back on the lot, the house retains ample privacy. The conversion from coach house to single-family home commonly occurred throughout this tour area. Several larger homes nestled in the middle of this block, visible to the west of the Kennedy House, also illustrate this trend (see 22).

20

9 Elizabeth

Patton and Fisher

Queen Anne

1888

converted into single-family dwelling, 1940

5 Elizabeth Court

Architect unknown

Italianate

c. 1875

21

a

George G. Mayo House 21 The Mayo House comprises a mixture and evolution of styles that mirror the rapid growth of the northwest section of Oak Park from the 1870s through 1910. It also bears the stamp of four different owners prior to 1908. Oak Park's proximity to Chicago generated an influx of settlers after the Chicago Fire of 1871. As early as 1872 Oak Park was becoming a suburb for the upper middle class and those of strong moral beliefs – Oak Park banned the sale of alcohol and built many churches (all mainstream Protestant religions were represented). In 1902 Oak Park prevented annexation to Chicago by breaking away from Cicero Township and becoming a self-governing independent village.

Reflective of changing tastes, this home elegantly demonstrates a juxtaposition of styles in consort; each adds sense and dignity to the whole. The L-shaped plan, low-sloped front-facing gable roof, and tall, narrow windows crowned with corbelled brick segmental arches are strong features that identify the original Italianate house. An English Tudor entry – with catslide roof and half-timbered side gable – and a simple one-story porch flank the original masonry structure. When architect L. D. Beman and his wife, Fanny, bought the property in 1891, they allegedly altered the interior considerably to reflect the early Prairie/indigenous-American style popularized by George W. Maher and E. E. Roberts.

The entry was probably updated in 1907 by then-owner F. J. McNish, who also removed a long side porch from the east end, extended the side gable into the catslide roof, and added the entry's round columns and Arts and Crafts-style carved beams and brackets. The vergeboard at the gables, a common Tudor Revival element, may have been added at this time as well.

Major H. M. and Margaret Robinson House  The dominant characteristics of the Robinson House exhibit an interwoven combination of the Queen Anne and Shingle styles. The front elevation, with simple gable, clapboard walls, and cornerboards, denotes the Queen Anne style. The rest of the building is more evocative of the Shingle style in its irregular and complex shapes contained within the protective shingle roofing, cantilevered side bay with overhanging gable, hipped dormer, and overall fluidity created by the textured shingled siding unrestricted by corner boards. The fusing of these two styles, whose popularity ran concurrently, occurred throughout Oak Park. Architects Patton and Fisher deftly handled this combination on a number of other buildings in the area.

The Robinsons sold the property to J. Fred and Lillie Butler in 1892, who lived in the house until 1917. The Butlers built a large two-story coach house at the rear of their expanded property in 1907. In 1956 the coach house was converted into a single-family dwelling, following the successful example of the Kennedy Coach House (see **20**).

22

3 Elizabeth

Patton and Fisher

Shingle style/ Queen Anne

1889

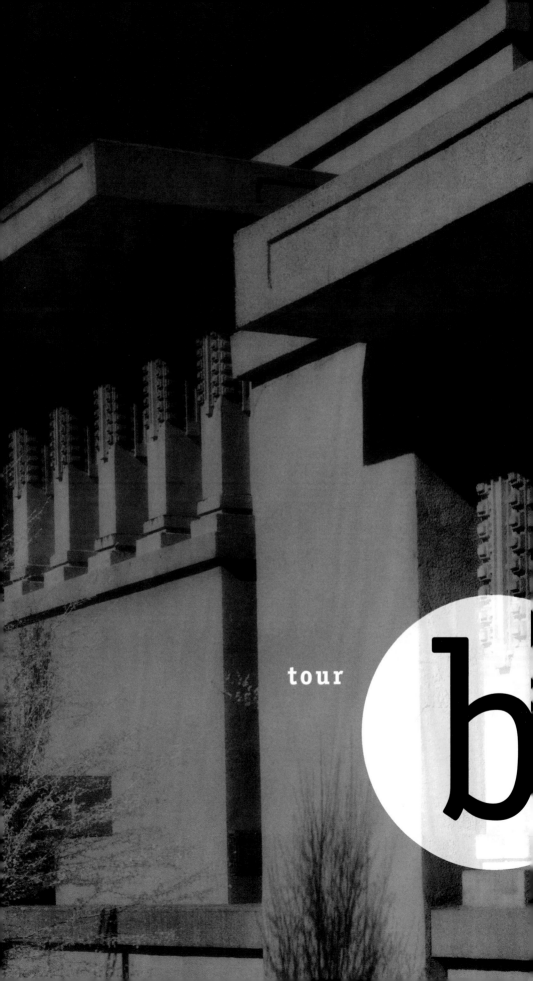

tour **b**

n

Chicago

Forest

28   29 30

27

31

33
34

32

26

25

Kenilworth

35   36

38

37

Elizabeth

24

23

39

Erie

Superior

46

Oak Park

45

start

Ontario

40

41

Grove

44

43

Lake

42

This tour combines many of the best-known buildings by Frank Lloyd Wright, some of the grandest late-nineteenth-century homes in the historic district, varied structures important to the history of apartment-building development, and several homes associated with figures of national importance. Unity Temple ④② is universally recognized as one of Wright's greatest creations, and the Hills-DeCaro home ②④ is a widely admired example of his early Prairie vision. Forest, Kenilworth, and Chicago Avenues include wonderful examples of the Prairie experiment, as well as such masterpieces of late-nineteenth-century wood-sided domestic architecture as the two Dunlop houses (③③ and ③④) by the most prolific and adaptable of local architects, E. E. Roberts.

161 North Grove ④① is one of the earliest surviving farmhouses, and 173-181 North Grove ④⓪, at the end of the same block, is an excellent example of the luxury courtyard buildings that developed in response to the pressure for apartment living in the downtown area of Oak Park. The apartments at 300–304 North Grove ③⑨ indicate not only the evolution of the courtyard building to the type occupying the full lot, but also the shift from revival styles to modernist Art Deco forms.

Doris Humphrey, the important ballet innovator, lived in one of the group of single-family homes at 303–319 North Grove ③⑧, and Ernest Hemingway was born in the Queen Anne home at 339 North Oak Park Avenue ④⑥, facts that, together with stylistic information, enable us to trace both the architectural and social history of the area on this tour.

tour

Tour B is approximately .9 miles

Estimated walking time 50 minutes

305 North
Forest

Architect
unknown

Stick style

c. 1885

23

Gordon Ripley House (23)   A splendid example of Victorian exuberance, this home may be distinguished as Stick style by its wide variety of applied woodwork. Unlike the earlier Gothic Revival style, which concentrated ornamental treatments around the windows and doors, here the wall surface is the primary vehicle for decoration. Thus, the carved and painted fan shapes, fishscale siding, cornerboards, painted bulls-eye decorations, and rich color scheme work to soften the rather simple underlying structure. Other distinctive features – such as the corner window fronted by a column; the Baroque-inspired, lathe-turned, bulbous double supports on the porch; and the pointed side chimney inscribed with a recessed arch – further complicate the house and point toward slightly later Queen Anne forms. With such varied gestures, the unknown architect was able to take full advantage of the corner site by carrying the visual effects around the building to the south facade.

Hills-DeCaro House  As a present to his daughter and son-in-law, Mary and Edward Hills, Nathan Moore arranged in 1906 to move this house dating from the mid-1880s from the south end of his property (see the Nathan Moore House ⑨). As part of this project, Moore commissioned Wright to renovate both the exterior and interior. Though the traditional two-story plan, entry porch, and high-pitched roofs reveal the earlier structure, Wright's emerging signature style is apparent in the deep, extended eaves. The home also features other early Prairie-style elements, including stucco walls, bands of windows, and geometric divisions achieved by the contrast of the stucco and wood trim accents. Inside, Wright designed built-in storage and decorative elements, and thus was able to make this home one of the earliest embodiments of his theory of an overall design that linked the interior and exterior. When a fire nearly destroyed the home in 1976, Irene and Thomas DeCaro acquired Wright's original plans and undertook in 1977 a complete reconstruction.

24

313 North Forest

Frank Lloyd Wright

Prairie style

1906

reconstructed 1977

318 North
Forest

Frank Lloyd
Wright

Prairie style

1902

25

Arthur Heurtley House 25   The Heurtley House design demonstrates
Frank Lloyd Wright's rapidly maturing Prairie School aesthetic, but also indicates the lingering influence of Wright's mentor, Louis Sullivan. The
substantial mass and grand scale of the building, as well as the doorway
arch, recall Sullivan's Auditorium Theater of 1887–89 and H. H. Richardson's
Glessner House of 1886. However, the Heurtley home – like its neighbor the
1901 Frank W. Thomas House 16 – also embodies strong Prairie-style elements; these include the raised living quarters, bands of windows,
ornamental art glass, and low-pitched hipped roof.

Because he was designing for an affluent client, Wright had the liberty to es-
chew the new, more economical stucco material for a brick exterior, which he
creatively used to emphasize the horizontal lines. The low brick wall partially conceals the entranceway and works against a direct approach to the
interior, an innovation that Wright played with throughout his career.
Another major concept in the evolution of the Prairie style is the harmony of
the interior and exterior. Here, the brick exterior and the arched entrance
are echoed in the great fireplace wall of the living room; and the continuous
windows along the main facade visually carry the underside of the roof into
the living and dining rooms. The unusually large lot, monumental proportions, massive roof, generous scale of the public spaces, and richness of
decoration create what has been classified justifiably as one of the great
homes of the early Prairie period. A total interior and exterior restoration in
1997–98 included revealing the original open porch.

Dr. William H. Copeland House  Wright's career accelerated rapidly in the five years before he left Oak Park in 1909, with major residential and commercial projects stretching from Montana to New York. One of the last commissions before his departure to Germany was another remodeling project for a neighbor. The earlier home was a severe cubic building that Wright changed by adding the open and enclosed porches, extending the eaves of the new roof, and redesigning the entire entranceway. He was also commissioned to remodel the public spaces of the first story, which enabled him to make a sympathetic transition from the exterior. By creating open, airy passageways and by using similar materials throughout, Wright subtly related the new doorway to the hallway inside. As a whole, the building exhibits a successful blend of elements from the earlier structure – such as the classical columns on the porch, which were already far removed from Wright's vocabulary by 1909 – with the more "Wrightian" entranceway and interior, forming a coherent and unique blend of Victorian and Prairie styles.

26

400 North
Forest

Frank Lloyd
Wright

Prairie style

remodeling
1908–1909

Chicago

Forest

28

27

26

Andrew Jackson Redmond House (27) Standing almost directly behind the two large homes the versatile Roberts designed for the Dunlop brothers ((33) and (34)), this slightly later house reflects a shift from such earlier examples of Victorian flourishes to sober respectability. It is one of the first of many houses E. E. Roberts designed with massive proportions, wide eaves, and broad porches, a step removed from the architect's earlier predilection for Queen Anne and Colonial Revival forms. This Renaissance-inspired house employs many striking elements – such as Palladian windows with Ionic columns, the great tile roof, and rich leaded glass over the prominent windows and doorway – that proclaim it a turn-of-the-century study in authority and wealth. The formality of the setting is further emphasized by the central walk, deep porch, symmetrical facade, and imposing wood entranceway framed by large stone porch piers. Enormous planters on the south side of the facade echo those that flank the stone front porch.

422 North Forest
E. E. Roberts
Eclectic
1900

27

931 Chicago
Architect unknown
Gothic Revival
c. 1866

28

Blair House (28) (not illustrated) This early Oak Park home was built in the Gothic Revival style popularized by Andrew Jackson Downing and illustrated in his builders' pattern books on domestic cottage architecture. Downing championed the Gothic Revival style as particularly suited to the American countryside, stressing that cottages in carefully designed landscapes promoted a morally superior lifestyle. Though Queen Anne-style lathe-turned spindles and fishscale siding now accent the facade, the steeply pitched gables and dormer, and the wall surface punctuated by tall, narrow windows, give the building a vertical emphasis that recalls the Gothic Revival style. A later addition of wings enlarged the house, and only the impressive ginkgo tree remains of the original landscape design.

The home had two owners of note: the well-known landscape gardener John Blair, who designed many Chicago parks and the estate of H. W. Austin in west Oak Park; and Wright's mother, Anna, whom he placed next door to his own home. The building now serves as the administrative offices of the Frank Lloyd Wright Home and Studio Foundation.

911 Chicago
E. E.
Roberts
Prairie style
1903–04

29

H. Benton Howard House ㉙   As part of a trend in which wealthy fathers commissioned houses for themselves and their children (see Wright's buildings for Nathan Moore, ⑨ and ㉔), Americus B. Melville built this home for his daughter and her husband one year before engaging Roberts to design his own house next door ㉚. One of Roberts's earliest explorations of Prairie-style elements as defined by Frank Lloyd Wright, this house represents a new direction taken by the prolific architect. Wright's influence can be seen particularly in the geometric divisions within the main section of the facade, the broad eaves of the hipped roof, and the strength of the central doorway and band of windows above it, all of which echo Wright's studio at the west end of the block. In combination with his exploration of the newer Prairie ideas, however, Roberts maintained late-Victorian elements that offset the more geometric arrangement of the facade. The frontal position of the chimney, the smaller, variously shaped side windows, and the irregular mixture of textures demonstrate the transitional nature of Roberts's design.

Americus B. Melville House  Indicating the range and adaptability of Roberts's residential work, this impressive house was built just one year after Americus B. Melville commissioned its smaller neighbor at 911 Chicago Avenue ㉙. Though Roberts often inserted his own version of the Prairie School vocabulary in his civic buildings, multi-unit complexes, and single-family homes, this house is one of the most Wright-influenced of the architect's career. In particular, the open interior – with the living room and dining areas that surround the impressive fireplace – echoes the early Prairie emphasis on the relationship between home and hearth. Additionally, the overall stucco finish and geometric massing are similar to Wright homes on the next block west. Nonetheless, Roberts created a stylistic tension in this house by including decoration such as the elongated Italianate bracketing, both outside and inside, and the interior arches, revealing his interest in historic revival architecture.

437 North Kenilworth

E. E. Roberts

Prairie style

1904

Charles E. Matthews House 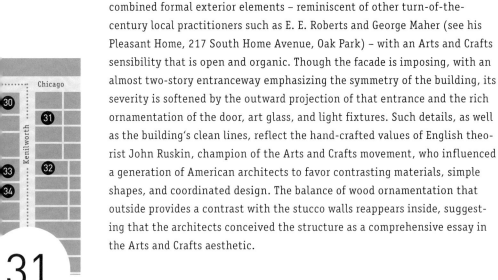 In this house Tallmadge and Watson combined formal exterior elements – reminiscent of other turn-of-the-century local practitioners such as E. E. Roberts and George Maher (see his Pleasant Home, 217 South Home Avenue, Oak Park) – with an Arts and Crafts sensibility that is open and organic. Though the facade is imposing, with an almost two-story entranceway emphasizing the symmetry of the building, its severity is softened by the outward projection of that entrance and the rich ornamentation of the door, art glass, and light fixtures. Such details, as well as the building's clean lines, reflect the hand-crafted values of English theorist John Ruskin, champion of the Arts and Crafts movement, who influenced a generation of American architects to favor contrasting materials, simple shapes, and coordinated design. The balance of wood ornamentation that outside provides a contrast with the stucco walls reappears inside, suggesting that the architects conceived the structure as a comprehensive essay in the Arts and Crafts aesthetic.

432 North Kenilworth

Tallmadge and Watson

Prairie style

1909

410 North
Kenilworth

Lawrence
Buck

Prairie style

1908

32

Edwin E. Ehrman House ③②   Lawrence Buck worked for George Maher before opening his own practice, and, like Maher, he designed Oak Park homes in the first decade of the twentieth century that are restrained essays inspired by the Arts and Crafts movement. Rather than manifesting Frank Lloyd Wright's increasingly modern vocabulary, this house exhibits the more traditional tendencies of the Arts and Crafts movement. Wright joined his windows with continuous sills and generally disliked using decoration under the eaves. In contrast, local Arts and Crafts buildings such as this one and the Tallmadge and Watson building up the street ③① are marked by flat stucco walls punctuated by discrete windows and embellished with darkly stained wood window trim. In addition, the Ehrman House has strong and distinctive ornamental brackets.

Ehrman built this home at a time when, as the Chair of the Building Committee, he was overseeing the construction of Unity Temple. It is possible that his frustration with the delays, cost overruns, and constant design changes of Unity Temple made him leery of engaging the same architect for his own home just a few blocks away.

417 North Kenilworth

E. E. Roberts

Queen Anne

1896

33

b

Simpson Dunlop House (33) A stately combination of classical details and the Queen Anne style, the Simpson Dunlop House, along with its neighbor at 407 North Kenilworth (34), represents a more conservative dimension of E. E. Roberts's widely diverse projects. The home, one of the largest in the area, stands on a sizable lot that accommodates a huge barn and coach house without any impact on the main structure.

Despite its striking vertical movement – produced by the extremely steep roof and tall third-floor windows – the building appears balanced and grounded in its setting. The large projecting front-facing gable and wide porch reflect the Queen Anne style; the double Ionic columns and pilasters, as well as the pediment over the porch, show the influence of classical revival styles; and the exaggerated pitch of the gables and dormers evokes a medieval feeling. The varied ornamentation derived from these eclectic sources contributes to the grandeur of the building.

Joseph Dunlop House  (34)   E. E. Roberts had the largest architectural practice in the history of Oak Park, with over 200 designs attributed to him. This house represents one of Roberts's basic "types," a large, handsome, and conservative essay in wooden architecture for the wealthy that displays various historical elements. Like the neighboring Simpson Dunlop home (33), this building is a Queen Anne structure in form that is decorated with classical ornamentation. One of the hallmarks of Roberts's success as a productive residential architect is the way he modified basic forms such as these to create visually distinct buildings. Thus, while the two homes have massing and plan in common, by using different porch configurations, changing the shape of the columns, and modifying the arrangement of the windows in the gables, Roberts was able to differentiate each one enough for it to appear an individual statement.

The scale of both houses, their imposing facades, and the impressive lots on which they stand, testify to the status and traditional tastes of the Dunlops.

34

407 North Kenilworth

E. E. Roberts

Queen Anne

1897

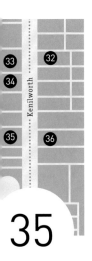

**317 North
Kenilworth**

**Patton and
Fisher**

Queen Anne

1893

William Douglass House 35   Designed by the firm of Patton and Fisher
in 1893, this large house is similar to the Dunlop homes E. E. Roberts built at
417 and 407 North Kenilworth several years later (33 and 34). Like many
1890s structures, this home exhibits Queen Anne features – a steep and irregular roofline, asymmetrical massing, and turned spindles on the porch –
combined with classically influenced details. Also of interest are the unique
and dramatic clusters of three columns, with smooth Tuscan shafts and capitals, on the porch and later porte cochere added in 1905. Though hardly rare,
dentils (notched moldings), which decorate both the first-and second-floor
cornices, are used here to excellent effect.

This home was built during Oak Park resident Normand Patton's most successful period, when he was building impressive churches, civic buildings,
and homes throughout this community and the city of Chicago.

H. P. Young House (36)   Of Wright's several remodeling jobs during his first years as an independent architect, this is the earliest documented example of his enlarging a home and changing its basic style. Young commissioned Wright, his neighbor, to modify his old farmhouse with a design that would be the equal of the grand homes in the area. Because the work took place simultaneously with Wright's design and construction of Nathan Moore's mansion (9), just a block away, it is not suprising that in this house Wright incorporated many of the same elements inspired by the Tudor Revival style. Like the Moore home, the Young House has tall, steeply pitched gables, diamond-paned casement windows, and wood timbering in the upper story. The Gothic-arched third-story window accentuates the medieval impression of the structure. But, as in many early Wright homes, other elements point to the architect's mature Prairie style: the grouped windows, severe rectilinear chimney, and, especially, the porte-cochere – created by the cantilevered extension of the porch roof – which permitted the family and guests to exit their carriages in inclement weather.

334 North Kenilworth

Frank Lloyd Wright

Tudor Revival

1895

36

b

**308 North
Kenilworth**

**Architect
unknown**

Stick style

1886

37

George B. Pratt House 37   This "painted lady," built by an unknown architect, is a fine example of the Stick style associated with New England homes of the previous decade. The style's characteristic emphasis on a highly decorated wall surface is handled superbly here, with some uncustomary features that supplement the normal range of detail and scroll-saw decorative applications. The contrast of plain clapboards with decorative shingles, combined with the paired, tapered porch supports at all corners, forms an unusually rich blend of ornament. The architect used wood strips to create geometric compartments of detailed areas in which fishscale and staggered shingles alternate, and at the peak of the gable is a beautiful screen with radiating rays. The whole upper section of the facade exhibits a rare balance between the areas so clearly delineated by the wooden strips and the curvaceousness of the ornamented screen and scroll-sawn applications.

Horton and Sharpe Speculation Houses  38 Developers Horton and
Sharpe hired architect E. E. Roberts to design these single-family homes in
1896. Together with a similar group of architect-designed homes – the Hales
Speculation Houses 77 up the street – these buildings are the only groups
of "spec" houses built in the district during this period. They reflect Oak
Park's growth and desirability as a neighborhood around the turn of the century and provide insight into early ideas regarding developer housing.

While based on simple, related plans, the houses are differentiated by
Roberts's skillful application of ornament borrowed from different styles. For
the most part, Roberts alternated between details derived from the Queen
Anne and the Tudor Revival styles. The one exception is 305 North Grove, in
which the simplified aesthetic and low, grounded quality suggest Prairie
School influences and thus a later design date.

Taken as a whole the development has a democratic quality – each house the
equal of the other. Their scale and proportions set the tone for the neighborhood and provide a wonderful historic foil to the nearby 1920s apartment
complex by the same architect 39 .

38

303–319
North Grove

E. E.
Roberts

Tudor
Revival/
Queen Anne

1896

39

**300–304
North Grove**

**E. E. and
Elmer
Roberts**

Art Deco

1926

Erie and Grove Apartments **39**   In the few years between the design of
this building and Roberts's courtyard apartments at 173–181 North Grove
40, it became possible to build "lot line to lot line" without setbacks or
courtyards. This upscale apartment building is a pioneering example of a new
form of multi-unit housing. It is also one of the few local residential Art Deco
buildings, a style particularly popular for commercial and civic architecture
throughout the United States in the 1920s and 1930s. Stylized and abstracted
natural and man-made forms, ornamental work inspired by the machine age,
and geometric motifs are hallmarks of the style. Distinctive Deco features of
this building include the decorative ironwork protecting the bay windows,
the oval windows, and the lit-glass address signs over the doorways. The in-
tegration of inlaid designs into the smooth masonry facades is also a Deco
feature.

Often the architect of choice throughout the thirty years he practiced in the
village, Roberts went through many evolutions as a designer, accepting the
best of each wave of architectural innovation – Queen Anne, Prairie, Colonial
Revival. He had taken his son into partnership some three years before they
designed this building. Increasing ill health had forced the designer into
semi-retirement when this building was nearing completion.

Parkview Apartments 40 (not illustrated)   This Tudor Revival building, from the period when apartment complexes that occupied entire lots came into existence, is one of the most richly decorated in Oak Park. Though initially there was public resistance to large, multi-unit family structures, the abundant light and air provided by the courtyards removed some of the objections of those who feared that these buildings would harbor disease. The presence of separate service entrances (on the Ontario side of the building) and multiple doorways, which allow for greater privacy, are hallmarks of an upper-middle-class rental experience that soon became an acceptable alternative to a single-family home.

In contrast to Roberts's later streamlined Art Deco design at 300–304 North Grove 39 , the decoration at Parkview is particularly rich, with armorial shields, quatrefoils, elaborate gargoyles, pointed Moorish arches in the entranceways, stone arches on the projecting bays, and stylized organic decoration at the roofline. An amusing touch is found at the service entrances, where the gargoyles are replaced by heads of workmen with their tools of trade.

173–181
North Grove

E. E.
Roberts

Tudor
Revival

1922

40

Hemingway's Second Home 41 (not illustrated)   While this building is of historic interest as the temporary home of young Ernest Hemingway and his family, it is equally important as one of the oldest surviving buildings in the community. Occupied continuously since 1870, it was for many years the residence of the pastors of the First Congregational Church, and later housed the offices of a series of medical professionals.

The building is a mid-century vernacular farmhouse, very likely constructed by a local builder rather than by an architect. What little ornamentation there is takes the form of simple surrounds on the tall and narrow windows. The house has been spared major modifications over the years. The interior appears to be in excellent original condition, and the most conspicuous exterior change is the enclosure of the porch on the north side of the home. Because this building has survived largely unchanged, it provides an indication of how early homes were constructed, as well as insight into the lifestyle of the area's pioneers.

161 North
Grove

Architect
unknown

Vernacular
farmhouse

c. 1870

41

Unity Temple 42   Built as the new home of the Universalist Congregation, whose former Gothic Revival building on Wisconsin Street was destroyed by fire in 1905, this innovative building of reinforced poured concrete has become one of the great landmarks of twentieth-century architecture.

The building actually consists of three parts: the auditorium, or chapel, in which the services are held; the general-purpose social hall; and the entrance hall, which opens to both the east and the west and serves to connect and separate the two major functional areas. It faces Kenilworth Avenue, rather than the thoroughfare street, Lake Street, thus turning its side to the noise and bustle of the streetcar and automobile. By making the visitor walk along the side of the building and turn ninety degrees to enter, Wright built up the drama and anticipation of seeing the actual space. He first used this design in domestic architecture in the Frank W. Thomas House of 1901 16 , and it was a device that he used throughout his career.

875 Lake
Frank Lloyd
Wright
Prairie style
1906–09

Conceived in volumetric modules, the building's two major sections are geometrically related, which enabled the builder to save money by reusing the expensive wooden construction forms for successive pours of the concrete. Inside, too, geometry acts as both the unifying and decorative concept. Stained wood strips outline and define rectilinear, plastered areas of colors that change in each section of the building. The colored glass in the coffers of the ceiling repeats the geometric decorative motif – a departure from the stylized plant forms found in Wright's early Prairie homes. Both the temple and the social hall – Unity House – are lit from above through the ceiling glass and the windows placed near the top of the wall, another device Wright used to cushion the congregation from the intrusive street.

Though the temple only houses 400 people in its four tiers of seating, the complex levels, stairs at each corner, interconnectedness of forms, and variety of colors and details all contribute to the impressiveness of what Wright referred to as the "Noble Room."

42

b

Ontario

40

41

Grove

Lake

42

43

Horse Show Fountain 43 (not illustrated)   The early history of the fountain is not clear, but it seems to have been a collaboration between Wright and Richard Bock, a talented sculptor who provided many of the decorations for Wright's studio and his other Oak Park commissions. The fountain, commissioned by the local Horse Show Association, was originally located farther west on Lake Street, at the curb, where it was accessible both to horses and people. At the time of the Wright centennial festivities, celebrated in Oak Park in 1969, the badly deteriorated concrete fountain was reconstructed and placed in its current setting. The rectilinear form, geometric planes, starkness of the concrete, and emphatic horizontal, projecting cap certainly reflect the aesthetics of Unity Temple, a block to the west, which was completed the same year that the fountain was executed. The low-lying planters (originally the horse troughs) on the two sides of the fountain – more severe in their geometry than the planters at either Unity Temple or Wright's own home – are a form that often appear in Wright's work.

44

Oak Park Club 44 (not illustrated)   The new Oak Park Club building was commissioned in 1922 as a gentleman's club that would emulate the downtown establishments favored by conservative businessmen. The selection of a firm with solid credentials as institutional architects was thus important. The partnership of Holmes and Flinn had already designed several other civic and religious buildings in Oak Park, including the First United Church at 848 Lake Street. In this building the solid and bold facade dominates the Ontario Street entrance, with an enormous pair of Corinthian columns at the top of the stairway. On the Oak Park Avenue side, the impressive arched windows of the public spaces, the pilasters with Corinthian capitals subtly recalling the columns on the Ontario side, and the modified Palladian windows refer to Italian Renaissance palazzos. By calling forth such classical associations, the architects successfully conveyed the status of their upper-class clientele.

The building, which once included bowling alleys, a swimming pool, bar, and dining room, was converted to condominiums in the early 1990s, and only the exterior and the main entranceway retain their original appearance.

Santa Maria Apartments 45 (not illustrated)   The Santa Maria
Apartments (now condominiums), one of the largest of its kind in the village,
has always been a coveted address, in large part due to the building's elaborate appearance and generously sized units. The complex includes two deep
courtyards and substantial areas of applied stone ornamentation in a variation of the Tudor Revival style that employed High Gothic details. In the
period immediately following World War I, antagonism to multi-unit structures that filled entire lots persuaded many builders to set the buildings back
from the street. The Santa Maria demonstrates another solution to the prob-
lem; while the building is constructed to the lot line, open spaces are created
through the innovation of deep courtyards. The street sides of the building
are richly decorated with shields, especially over the projecting bays, and or-
nate canopies inspired by Gothic cathedrals hang over the corners closest to
Oak Park Avenue. Moving into the courtyards, the ornamentation, crowned
by pinnacles and trefoils, becomes even more complex, but all of the parts
are united through the creamy-toned stone and terracotta trim that divides
the brickwork.

45

**208–232
North Oak
Park and
719–739
Erie**

**Architect
unknown**

**Tudor
Revival**

1924

Hemingway Birth Home Designed by a little-known architect, Wesley Arnold, this Queen Anne home is famous as the birthplace of Ernest Hemingway, whose maternal grandparents, Ernest and Caroline Hall, purchased the lot in 1889. The future writer was born on July 21, 1899, in the south bedroom of the home. The family remained here until the death of Grandfather Hall, whose will stated that the home be sold to provide for his wife and children.

Typical of Queen Anne structures, the house once had a porch with a spindled railing that wrapped around the front and south sides. The wood clapboard siding, asymmetrical massing, turret surmounting the bedroom at the southeast corner, and fishscale siding that accents the attic level of the turret are also classic expressions of the style. The original paint scheme was medium gray, with dark gray trim and deep green window surrounds.

Now opened and operated by the Ernest Hemingway Foundation, the Hemingway Birth Home is open for tours at regular hours.

46

339 North Oak Park

Wesley Arnold

Queen Anne

1890

tour

C

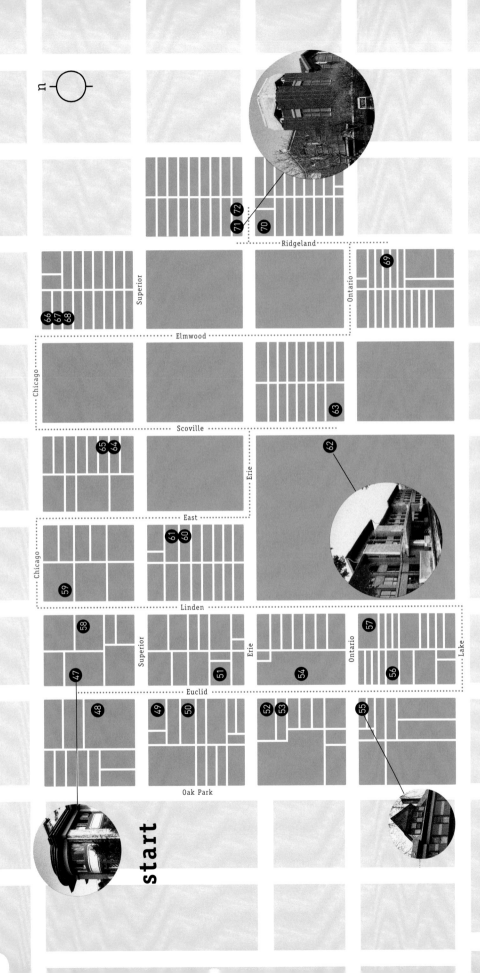

N

Ridgeland

Superior

Ontario

Elmwood

Chicago

Scoville

Erie

East

Chicago

Linden

Superior

Erie

Ontario

Lake

Euclid

Oak Park

start

In the diverse buildings on this tour – including a church, high school, apartment house, and numerous residences – it is possible to see the evolution of Oak Park from a fledgling suburban retreat to a dense community. The structures discussed here range from 1880 to 1920, though most were designed between 1900 and 1915. This time period includes the building boom after the 1871 Chicago Fire and the economic prosperity of the pre-World War I era. The men who commissioned the buildings were the industrial and commercial leaders of the Chicago area, and the architects they chose range from the famous (Frank Lloyd Wright) to the almost unknown (A. L. Moody).

The tour covers buildings between the north/south streets of Euclid Avenue and Ridgeland Avenue, and the east/west streets of Chicago Avenue and Lake Street in the present Village of Oak Park. Most of this area was the Village of Ridgeland from the 1870s until 1902, when Oak Park separated from Cicero Township and absorbed Ridgeland. From 1880 to 1920, the population of Oak Park grew from 1,812 to 36,585.

In the early-twentieth century, two-and three-flat buildings with exteriors that mimicked single-family houses were the favored solution to the increased housing requirements. After World War I, in response to issues of unregulated growth, architect Charles White developed a local zoning ordinance. The Oak Park zoning law (based on the newly passed state zoning law) was enacted in 1921 and included areas zoned for multi-unit housing. Although resisted by many as changing the character of the village, by the mid-1920s upscale apartments such as the Linden Apartments 57 were under construction. A building depression between 1930 and 1950, caused by the Great Depression and World War II, created a severe housing shortage in the village. As a result many single-family houses were subdivided into multiple-family flats or were converted to rooming houses. Today most of these structures have been restored to their original single-family status, reflecting Oak Park's desirability as an upscale neighborhood.

tour

C

Tour C is approximately 2.4 miles

Estimated walking time 135 minutes

Charles Ward Seabury House 47 (not illustrated)   Charles White's design of this brick and stucco house with a slate roof draws on the Tudor Revival style, derived from medieval English houses and popular in America from 1890 to 1940. White's choice of the Tudor Revival style indicates his shift away from the Prairie School. In the Seabury House the steeply pitched gable roofs and decorative half-timbering on the two projecting bays recall the country houses of English nobility. Such allusions made the style popular in affluent communities for clients like Charles Ward Seabury, an officer of the insurance brokerage firm Marsh and McLennan. Seabury was also active in the YMCA and other cultural, health, and educational organizations in the Chicago area. Richard W. Sears, founder of Sears Roebuck and Company, had formerly owned the land and had intended to build a house designed by George Maher on the site.

47

420 North
Euclid

Charles E.
White, Jr.

Tudor
Revival

1912

James Hall Taylor House

James Hall Taylor House 48   The Taylor House, Maher's last commission in Oak Park, is representative of the architect's unique interpretation of the Prairie style, which he introduced in 1897 in his design of Pleasant Home (217 Home Avenue). Here the masonry facade has a smooth, uncluttered quality that conveys a feeling of solidity and formality. A segmental arch, an element favored by Maher during this period, appears over the front door and again in the shape of the south bay. This feature creates the image of a sculptured building that nicely accommodates the low-pitched, hipped tile roof, overhanging eaves, and bands of windows. Flower planters beside the substantial front entrance, tall chimneys, and small columns on the second floor above the entrance add to the formal arrangement of the structure. Unity Church of the Daily Word purchased the building in 1965; its members removed a pergola and garage in 1971 in order to build a sanctuary to the west of the house. James Hall Taylor, an official at Taylor Forge and Pipe Works, was active in local Presbyterian church affairs. He lived in the house until his death in 1951.

405 North Euclid

George W. Maher

Prairie style

1912

48

C

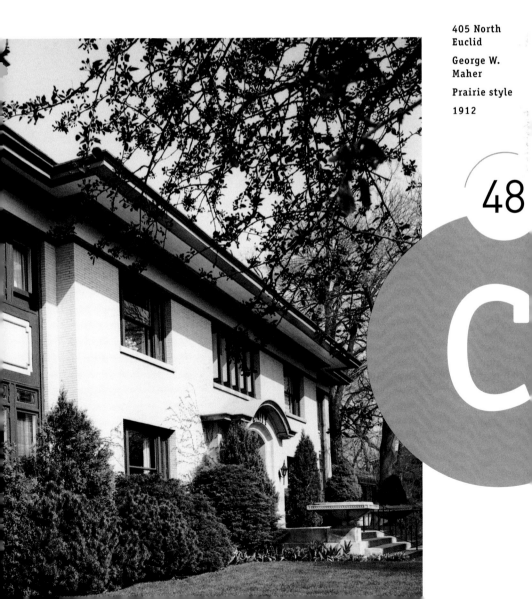

Paul Blatchford House III 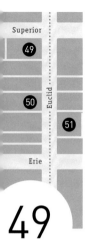 The Blatchfords' previous house, originally on this site, was moved one block east to make room for this residence. As major proponents of the Arts and Crafts movement, architects Irving and Allen Pond chose to focus on English cottage architecture as the inspiration for this early design, one of the firm's few excursions into residential architecture. Simplicity, rhythm, and an honest use of materials characterize the building. The lower floors of red brick are juxtaposed against the shingled upper portion; half-timber details embellish the front bay; and half-circle hoods define the front entrance roof and dormers.

Naming their new home "Plasderw" – Welsh for "house among the oaks" – the family of six, along with eight servants, moved in during March of 1898. Frances Lord Blatchford brought the boulder in the front yard from her home in Bangor, Maine. Mr. Blatchford was active in Blatchford and Company's lead works in Chicago. He later became secretary of the Central Supply Association, which was made up of manufacturers and jobbers of water, steam, and gas supplies.

49

333 North Euclid

Pond and Pond

Eclectic

1898

321 North
Euclid

Burnham
and Root

Queen Anne

1883 or
1885

Frank Lloyd
Wright

Prairie style

interior
remodeling
1896

50

Charles E. Roberts House 50   Burnham and Root, one of the pioneers of the Chicago School of architecture, designed many office buildings, churches, and houses, especially in Chicago, between 1873 and 1892. This Queen Anne house (now much changed) with decorative curved half-timbering is one of the few Oak Park examples of a residence designed by that firm.

In 1896 Frank Lloyd Wright remodeled the interior of the house for Charles E. Roberts, an industrialist who invented an electric automobile and established the Chicago Screw Company. A member of the church board that commissioned Wright to build Unity Temple in 1906, he was an early supporter of the young architect's innovations. Wright's burgeoning skill at interior design is clearly apparent in this home, particularly in the ornamental woodwork. The spindled staircase, the cabinet with perforated oak screen over the fireplace, and the art glass in several places are striking rectilinear features that anticipate his later preoccupation with such forms. The present porch, a recent addition, is in the same vein as Wright's remodeling.

312 North
Euclid

Patton and
Miller

Colonial
Revival

1903

51

Calvin H. Hill House 🔵51　　In the first decade of the twentieth century, historically accurate versions of the Colonial Revival style (1880–1950) were in vogue, as exemplified by this design based on Federal architecture, an English style brought over to the colonies and popular between 1780 and 1840. The symmetrical facade emphasizing the central pedimented entry, Palladian dormer windows, and the central window crowned with a broken pediment are all features that might be found on an early-nineteenth-century Federal house. The stable/garage/apartment on the alley side of the lot was built in 1904. During the period between 1930 and 1950, when there was a nationwide building depression and a housing shortage in Oak Park, this residence was turned into a rooming house. Calvin Heywood Hill, the original owner, opened the Midwest branch of Heywood-Wakefield Furniture Company. Mr. Hill served as Oak Park Village President, as well as president of the West Suburban Hospital Association and other local organizations.

Edward W. McCready House 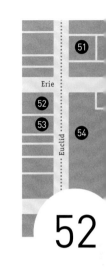 The house Robert C. Spencer, Jr., designed for Edward McCready, manager and treasurer of the R. W. McCready Cork Company, is a solid and formal version of the architect's mature Prairie style. The stone beltcourse, low-pitched hipped roof, and exterior tan Roman brick with raked joints emphasize the building's horizontal lines, a characteristic of the Prairie style. Spencer began his Chicago-area practice in 1894 and built his own home in River Forest in 1905; from 1905 to 1923, Horace Powers was his partner. Their designs in River Forest and Oak Park dating from 1907 to 1915 exhibit the same substantial masses as the McCready House. In addition to his design work, Spencer wrote extensively about architecture and invented casement-window hardware.

Mr. McCready's widow, Caroline Pitkin McCready, continued to live in the house until her death in 1957. She was active in community organizations such as the Economy Shop and the League of Women Voters.

231 North Euclid

Spencer and Powers

Prairie style

1907

223 North
Euclid

Frank Lloyd
Wright

pre-Prairie

1897

53

George W. Furbeck House 53 (not illustrated)   George Furbeck commissioned this experimental house, with its complex interplay of geometric shapes and textured brick patterns, from Frank Lloyd Wright early in his career. It is the first of several buildings Wright designed over a three-year period that led him to the Frank W. Thomas House of 1901 4 , his first full-blown Prairie structure in Oak Pak. In the Furbeck House he combined Queen Anne octagonal towers and Japanese-influenced splayed eaves over the porch with features that point to his mature Prairie style, such as the high beltcourse, the wide overhanging eaves, and the prominent rectangular chimney. The many changes made to the building over the years include the garage and back porch additions (1920) and the enlargement and enclosure of the front porch (1922). The third-floor and kitchen remodeling occurred in 1950.

George Furbeck was treasurer of the Chicago Lithostone Company. The house was a wedding present from his father, Warren Furbeck, who was a banker/broker/street railroad company officer.

220 North
Euclid

White and
Christie

Tudor
Revival

1913

54

Caswell A. Sharpe House (Cheney Mansion) 54 (not illustrated)   This Tudor Revival building replaced an 1880s Shingle-style house on the same site, also belonging to C. A. Sharpe. The reinforced concrete structure is faced with red Roman brick. The development of this facing technique – a significantly cheaper alternative to solid brick or stone construction – led to a rapid rise in the popularity of the Tudor Revival style in the 1920s and 1930s. An earlier design for this house illustrated an article by White entitled "What Should I Expect from My Architect," published in *House Beautiful* (June, 1913). It shows a more elaborate Tudor Revival structure with two bays and a different interior plan. As built, the brick exterior, steep roof, and strong gable with a hint of half-timbering express typical features of the Tudor Revival style. Additions include the brick garage with an apartment above (1914) and the sun porch (1922). The greenhouse (1924) was built by the well-known firm of Lord and Burnham of Des Plaines, Illinois. When the last owner, Mary Dole, died, the property passed to her niece Elizabeth Cheney, who deeded the property to the Park District of Oak Park when she died in 1985.

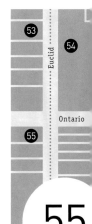

55

175 North
Euclid
A. L. Moody
Queen Anne
1886–87

Robert J. Adamson House ⑤⑤ The abundant detailing and commanding presence of this home evoke an era of prosperity when Midwestern industry created a new class of wealth. Large Queen Anne structures such as this one – built for Mr. Adamson of Bader and Adamson, a large glue manufacturing firm – were typical in Oak Park. The heavily decorated wall surface (a characteristic of the Stick style that was continued in the Queen Anne style) features curved and triangular cut shingles, beveled lap siding, and vertical bead board below the cornice. The uninterrupted flow of the wall cladding around the corners is a Shingle-style treatment common in Oak Park homes of this period.

Changing community demographics are reflected in the building's history: Jacob Mortensen, the second owner and a prominent lumberman, added the heavy front porch in 1916; between 1935 and 1940, the building was used as a rooming house; later it was divided into two-family apartments, and a garage was added; at some point, the coach house was developed into a separate residence (715 Ontario). The house has since been returned to a single-family residence.

Henry P. Magill House Roberts designed this substantial Prairie-style house for insurance executive H. P. Magill. The building – with hipped roof, deep eaves, broad front porch, and symmetrical arrangement – recalls George Maher's formal Prairie structures, particularly his Pleasant Home at 217 Home Avenue. The break in the roofline to accommodate the central second-floor windows, which are highlighted with Sullivanesque decorative carving, interrupts the horizontality of the design. Between 1903 and 1912 Roberts produced a number of such monumental houses featuring stucco walls and broad porches; a similar, though more simple, house of this type built in 1907, can be found at 224 South Ridgeland Avenue. The south wing of the house probably was added in 1916, the second floor of which was built after 1979.

Roberts established his practice in 1893, and his son Elmer served as his partner from 1923 to 1926. His popular and successful Oak Park practice was the largest in the village.

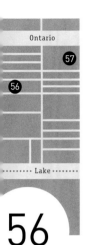

56

164 North Euclid

E. E. Roberts

Prairie style

1903

175–181
Linden/
643–645
Ontario

John S. Van
Bergen

Prairie style

1915–16

Linden Apartments 57   Van Bergen began designing the Prairie-style Linden apartment building in 1915 for Salem E. Munyer, a linens importer and distributer who commissioned the building but never lived there. To ensure the maximum amount of light and air, Van Bergen gave every one of the eighteen apartments – each having four, five, or six rooms – a glazed and screened front porch and a rear sleeping porch. All but the smallest apartments have fireplaces, and the rear fire escape is enclosed, an innovation for the time. The main entrance is arranged in a "V" shape so there are six corner apartments instead of three. The raked mortar joints of the buff-colored Roman brick walls, as well as the limestone lintels and sills, emphasize the horizontal plane, which Van Bergen balanced through the vertical lines of the windows, chimneys, and piers of the main entrance.

Van Bergen, an Oak Park native and former student of Wright, had his own architectural firm from 1911 to 1968. He designed Prairie-style buildings mainly in Oak Park, Highland Park, and Santa Barbara, California.

57

C

**415 North
Linden**

**Tallmadge
and Watson**

Prairie style

1912

Gustavus Babson House II (58) Six years after designing Gustavus Babson's first house in Oak Park (118), Tallmadge and Watson gave him this second house, a more elaborate and imposing Prairie-style structure of red brick and stucco trimmed in stone. The engaged vertical piers that support the gabled roof are considered to be a trademark of Tallmadge and Watson designs. Also common are the peaked windows that extend into the gable. The sun parlor was added in 1916 and the garage in 1917. The brick and stucco addition of 1929 included a second-story bedroom and three bathrooms. During the 1960s the building stood vacant for three years, causing demolition to be considered by the village. Fortunately, the Poplett family bought the house in 1967 and restored it to its original form.

Thomas E. Tallmadge and Vernon Watson were partners from 1905 to 1936. Tallmadge also taught, wrote architecture books, and served on the Architectural Commission for the Restoration of Colonial Williamsburg. Watson designed his own house on Fair Oaks Avenue (112).

Julius Fred Butler House 59 (not illustrated)   Charles E. White and Louis R. (sometimes cited as Charles) Christie designed this elaborate red brick Colonial Revival house in 1915 for the Butlers, who moved in during 1917, christening the house "Twin Oaks." The austere columns, prominent dentils under the roofline, and smooth stone detail over the south-facing front door imitate the eighteenth-century colonial Georgian style. In his career White employed a number of styles, ranging from Prairie to historic revival (see 94 and 47). His Prairie designs were probably influenced by his experience working in Frank Lloyd Wright's studio from 1903 to 1905.

Around 1915 Mr. Butler commissioned the firm to build a house for his daughter and her husband at 414 North Linden. From 1918 to 1921, the Butlers increased their property to 2.2 acres, purchasing land along Linden, Chicago, and East Avenues. Though much of that land was later sold and other houses were built on it, the south-facing Butler house still looks out onto gardens while turning its back to busy Chicago Avenue. His earlier Oak Park residence still stands at 3 Elizabeth Court 22 .

440 North
Linden

White and
Christie

Colonial
Revival

1915

59

William Lees House I 60   William Lees engaged Charles E. White, Jr., to design this house of red brick and stucco with an attendant garage. The house shows White's interest in Tudor-style English cottage architecture, a subject about which he wrote extensively and to which he often referred in practice. The general massing and asymmetrical window groupings are similar to White's design for Lees's property at 321 North East Avenue 61 . The design, inspired by the forms of medieval English folk cottages rather than stately manor houses, features multi-paned windows and a dominant front-facing gable interrupted by a prominent chimney. The style was most popular in the 1920s and 1930s, when new masonry veneering techniques allowed architects to imitate the brick and stone exteriors of the English prototypes. A sleeping porch was added in 1933.

325 North
East

White and
Christie

Tudor
Revival

1919

60

William Lees House II  (not illustrated)   William Lees, president of the William Lees Heating Company, commissioned this two-story house from Charles E. White, Jr., as an investment property. White also built Mr. Lees's own house a year earlier on the lot to the north ⓺⓪. Several features here suggest the influence of English cottage designs, including the second-floor overhang supported by brackets above the front door and the combination of red brick and stucco. Though White worked in Frank Lloyd Wright's office and designed in a number of styles, he wrote about English domestic architecture and seemed particularly interested in adapting its forms to the American landscape.

The first occupants of this house, according to the early directories, were Warren S. and Grace Hill Corning. Mr. Corning dealt in railway supplies, and Mrs. Corning was the daughter of F. A. Hill, builder and real-estate broker.

321 North East

White and Christie

Tudor Revival

1920

Superior

61
60

East

Scoville

62   63

Ontario

62

Oak Park and River Forest High School

The Scoville and East Avenue sides are the only visible pieces of the earliest buildings in this complex; these secondary facades are the finest large masonry walls in Oak Park. River Forest resident Robert Spencer and Oak Parker Normand Patton shared the commission for the first building to be located on Ontario Street from Scoville Avenue to East Avenue. The L-shaped block at Ontario and Scoville was built in 1906, followed in 1908 by the East Avenue/Ontario Street corner. The main entrance on Ontario Street was obliterated by the 1968 addition connecting the school and gyms. Despite these changes, the pieces added to the north between 1908 and 1924 follow the original design and blend in smoothly.

Patton already had many school and university projects to his credit, including several dozen designed when he was chief architect for the Chicago Board of Education in 1897 and 1898. Spencer's practice, on the other hand, was largely residential. Though the drawings traveled back and forth between the two architects' offices, the resemblance to the other work of Patton's firm suggests that his office was primarily responsible for the design.

Much of Patton's best early work was in a robust Richardsonian Romanesque style. Chicago architects including Louis Sullivan and John Wellborn Root experimented during the 1880s and 1890s with modern interpretations of this style's wall type, often sheathing a steel frame with brick. The high school shows the evolution of this wall organization. A firm base in a contrasting color supports three floors topped by a row of round arched windows, but instead of large blocks of masonry, the finely detailed wall is of pressed brick. Acorns and oak leaves, in the Arts and Crafts style, decorate the plaques at the fourth-floor level, while a low hipped roof with wide eaves adds Prairie-style horizontal emphasis. Before his 1913 addition on Erie Street, E. E. Roberts had used this vocabulary in his 1908 Scoville block (137 North Oak Park Avenue).

Intense overcrowding and a limited availability of land forced the placement of Everett I. Brown's 1968 infill addition across Ontario Street and against the original facade. The current entrances show none of the charm of the old entryway, fragments of which have been reinstalled along the Scoville Avenue facades.

- Alice Sinkevitch

201 North Scoville

1906, Normand S. Patton and Robert C. Spencer, Jr.

1908, 1911 Patton and Miller

1913, Erie Street addition, E. E. Roberts

1921, Holmes and Flinn

1924, Perkins, Fellows and Hamilton

1968, Everett I. Brown and Associates

Prairie style

200 North
Scoville

Tallmadge
and Watson

Prairie style

1909

63

Torrie S. Estabrook House 63   In 1909 Canadian-born Torrie Estabrook, an officer of the lumber company bearing his name, engaged Tallmadge and Watson to build this one-and-a-half-story stucco and shingle Prairie-style bungalow. The cruciform plan, with the living room and dining room separated by the fireplace and aligned down the center of the building, resembles Frank Lloyd Wright's Robie House (in Hyde Park), also of 1909, although on a much smaller scale. The garage in the basement at the back of the house, unusual for a residence of this period, indicates the rising influence of the automobile on house design. Although the windows on the front facade are not peaked – a frequent feature in the firm's houses of this period – the plentiful use of wood trim, particularly in the gable, clearly identifies the design as Tallmadge and Watson's. An unusual feature, somewhat obscured in the photograph above, is the double-gabled roof on the side wing.

407 North
Scoville

Tallmadge
and Watson

Prairie style

1915

64

C

Joseph S. Guy House II (64)   Built in 1915 this two-story red-brick home
is one of the last Prairie-style designs by the firm. Their late use of a waning
style is probably due, in part, to the fact that the client, English-born
Joseph Guy, was a partner in the contracting firm of Guy and McClintock,
which built many Prairie-style buildings in Oak Park and River Forest. After
forming a partnership in 1905, Tallmadge and Watson developed their own
distinct version of the Prairie style – the young architects were influenced
by Frank Lloyd Wright although they never worked in his studio. Between
1906 and 1916 the firm designed a large number of houses that exhibit many
of the features found here: engaged piers, grouped windows, and wide projecting eaves. After World War I the firm turned to revival styles, exemplified
by the Georgian Revival house at 506 North Euclid Avenue, and in the 1920s
the partnership received many ecclesiastical commissions.

Joseph S. Guy House I  The wide variety of Tallmadge and Watson buildings in this guidebook provides an opportunity to compare and contrast their often recognizable designs. The previous house on this tour, the Guy II House, appears more compact and grounded than this design – in part because here the peaked windows project into the gables and add vertical movement to the facade. A feature in this house that differentiates it from the Guy II House is the facade's symmetry – suggested by the centered porch – that resembles the Carroll House (111), also built in 1913. The house was constructed on speculation for Joseph Guy two years before his own house was built (see (64)). Because the first occupant was Frederick B. Mathis, a sales manager, the residence is sometimes referred to as the Mathis House. In 1914 a garage was added, and in 1935 Charles Kristen designed a brick and stucco addition for the house.

411 North Scoville

Tallmadge and Watson

Prairie style

1913

426 North Elmwood

432 North Elmwood

436 North Elmwood

68

Flori Blondeel Houses 66, 67, 68   The three Prairie-style houses of stucco with wood trim accents were designed by Van Bergen for a local florist, Flori Blondeel. In 1913 Van Bergen designed 426 North Elmwood with no thought of it as the beginning of a formal group. However, the two other commissions quickly followed. Van Bergen used Frank Lloyd Wright's "Fireproof House for $5,000" (see also 98, 99, and 100) as the basis for the middle house at 432, and reversed the plan of the first house for 436 North Elmwood. He was clearly unaware that he was going to receive the commission for the second two houses, because he had already sold the design for 436 North Elmwood to another client in Oak Park (William Griffith, at 418 South Harvey). In the end, these three houses on Elmwood make a distinct ensemble. While they stand relatively close together, the sight lines and window placements are such that the residents' privacy is maintained. Perhaps due to World War I, the houses did not sell immediately, and the first residents were renters.

167 North Ridgeland
Spencer and Powers
Prairie style
1909

69

William C. Stephens House 69 (not illustrated)   While the building gives the impression it is Tudor Revival style because of its steep roof and half-timbered exterior, Robert C. Spencer, Jr., really designed a handsomely proportioned Prairie-style house. Exterior features of Tudor Revival (1890–1940) and Prairie-style (1900–1920) buildings often appear similar. Here Tudor Revival "half-timbering" doubles as Prairie-style "wood trim" that divides the upper story into geometric sections (see Tallmadge and Watson's designs in 82, 96, and 111). What best differentiates the two styles is the Prairie School's innovations regarding the interior plan and total design of a building. In this house the interior features large rooms flowing one into another and bathed in natural light from the many windows. Attention to the design as a whole is expressed in the built-in cabinets, large storage areas, and stylized floral and geometric designs in the art-glass windows. Some original light fixtures and casement-window hardware invented by Spencer are still in place. The house was built for English-born William Charlton Stephens, who was associated with hardware manufacturing.

232 North Ridgeland
E. E. Roberts
Prairie style
1912

70

Burt S. Davis House 70 (not illustrated)   Designed in 1912 by E. E. Roberts, this handsome stucco Prairie-style house was built for Burt S. Davis, a longtime Marshall Fields traveling salesman. The horizontal lines often associated with the Prairie style are expressed in the overhanging eaves, hipped roof, bands of windows connected by continuous sills, and wide front porch. At the time these were favorite features of Roberts, who designed hundreds of homes in River Forest and Oak Park, where he lived and maintained an office during most of his career. The houses Roberts designed at 422 North Forest 27, 533 North Grove 75, and 524 North Oak Park 81 are other examples of this type, ranging in date from 1900 to 1912. In these designs Roberts varied almost identical rectilinear forms by applying different types of dormers, porches, entranceways, and other decorative features. Davis also owned the properties at 226 North Ridgeland and 319 Erie, which also may have been designed by E. E. Roberts.

Trinity Lutheran Chapel and Church

71

72

Trinity Lutheran Chapel and Church (71), (72)   The chapel and church, built seven years apart, reflect the fate that befell the Prairie style during these pivotal years. In 1909 E. E. Roberts designed a Prairie-style chapel on Erie Street for the Trinity Lutheran congregation. The original plan, to convert the chapel into a parsonage when the church was later built, was never carried out. In 1916 Roberts built the red brick church facing Ridgeland Avenue. Though changing tastes persuaded Roberts to employ outwardly Gothic forms for the church building, he maintained the Prairie style in their expression, exemplified by the geometric shapes and placement of the windows, the building's massing that echoes the original chapel, and the stringcourse above the entrance doors that emphasizes the horizontal in the Prairie-style manner. Sadly, the chapel was changed both inside and outside to accommodate church activities and to relate the exterior to the later Gothic-style church Roberts built next door. The chapel's stucco facade on Ridgeland was covered with brick, and the door – originally approached through an open porch on Erie Street – was moved to the opposite side, destroying the balance of the original Prairie facade.

**300 North
Ridgeland**

E. E. Roberts

Prairie style

1909

**Gothic
Ecclesiastical**

1916

tour

d

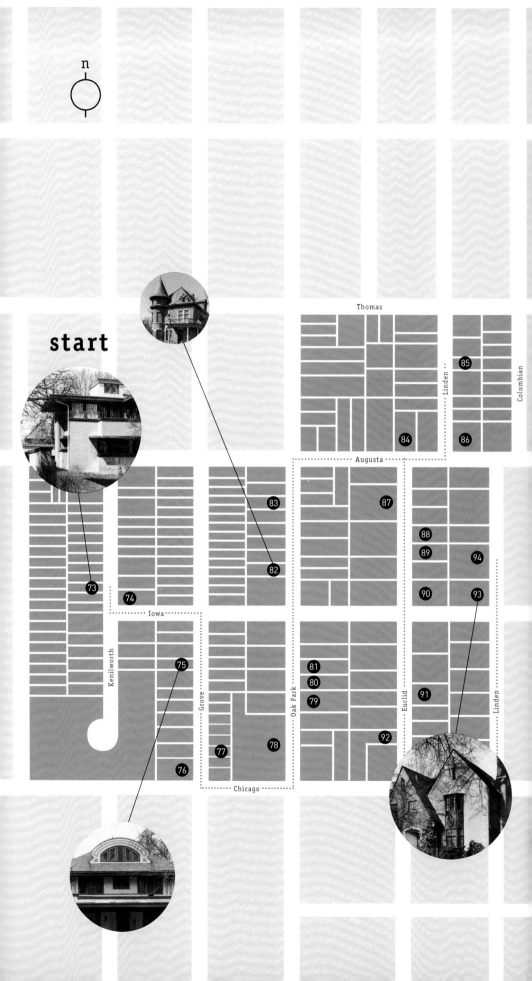

start

Thomas

Linden

Columbian

85

84

86

Augusta

87

83

88

89

94

82

90

93

73

74

Iowa

Kenilworth

75

81

Grove

Oak Park

80

Euclid

91

Linden

79

77

78

92

76

Chicago

Wright's last two Prairie designs built in Oak Park afford the opportunity to contrast his work with the other Prairie architects – Henry Holsman, George Maher, E. E. Roberts, Tallmadge and Watson, and Charles E. White. The work of E. E. Roberts, one of Oak Park's most productive architects – with over 200 designs attributed to him – comprises diverse building styles; he was inclined more, perhaps, than Wright to listen to the client.

The housing stock on this tour runs the architectural gamut, with work by eleven architects ranging from 1880s Stick style to 1920s revivals. Oak Park's first houses were built on the land immediately to the north and south of the Galena and Chicago (now Union Pacific) railroad tracks. The area on this tour represents the expansion of the village to a second section as dictated by population growth. Old farms were divided, and the houses were replaced by architect-designed homes, although a few farmhouses remain. One remnant of earlier rural days, 638 North Kenilworth, is down the block from Wright's Balch House **73** of 1911.

tour

d

Tour D is
approximately
1.8 miles

Estimated
walking time
90 minutes

611 North
Kenilworth

Frank Lloyd
Wright

Prairie style

1911

73

Oscar B. Balch House 73   One of Wright's first commissions after returning from Europe, this stucco and wood house was designed for a local interior decorator. Wright had spent two years in Berlin preparing a portfolio of his work for publisher Ernst Wasmuth. In the Balch house he employed his usual architectural vocabulary – a flat roof with broad eaves, wide chimney, hidden side entry, and ribbon windows (a series of windows forming a horizontal band). The design also includes a small balcony on the second floor. Certain similarities to the brick Edwin Cheney design of 1903 104 can be seen as well: the living areas have windows on three sides, and the living room opens onto a front terrace, integrating the exterior and interior spaces. Although Wright did not like basements, and discontinued incorporating them in his later houses, this 1911 house has a deep basement. The original stucco was tinted light gray, with the wood trim in contrasting red. Balch, the owner, sold the house in 1920.

Clarence E. and Grace Hall Hemingway House 74   Grace Hemingway collaborated with architect Henry Fiddelke on this stucco four-square design, a common vernacular version of the Prairie style featuring a square or rectangular plan, low-pitched hipped roof, and symmetrical facade. The music room (now demolished) where Grace gave music lessons and held family parties was designed according to her suggestions, as were the office spaces of Dr. Hemingway. Patients would enter the offices, which included an examining room, waiting room, and laboratory, through a broad, open front porch on the west facade; the bay windows on the south side indicate where the waiting room was located. The diamond-shaped leaded glass windows and small rear balcony enliven an otherwise simple exterior. A plaque on the front lawn designates this house as the home of Ernest Hemingway from 1906 until he graduated from Oak Park high school in 1917. On the third floor, he wrote his first stories for the high school newspaper and in the fall of 1917 he took a job as a cub reporter at the *Kansas City Star*.

74

600 North Kenilworth

Henry G. Fiddelke

Prairie style

1906

Louis H. Brink House

75

Grove

77

76

Chicago

Louis H. Brink House ⑦⑤   The popularity of stucco is evident in most of E. E. Roberts's work, earning him the title of "stucco king." This handsome example of the architect's oeuvre is a tribute to his ability to translate the Prairie style into his own vocabulary. The house has too much "muscle" to be considered purely Prairie, and the four curvilinear dormers distinguish this design from the others Roberts built in Oak Park during this period (see ㉗, ⑦⓪, and ⑧①). Also interesting is the mixture of casement and double-hung windows and the linear ornamentation on the front facade and north, side facade. In the interior Roberts incorporated dark-stained wood trim and leaded glass (in both Prairie and Art Nouveau styles) in the doors, windows, lighting fixtures, and built-ins. The original owner operated Brink and Sons, an established produce and commission house in Chicago.

533 North Grove
E. E. Roberts
Prairie style
1909

75

503 North Grove
Patton and Fisher
Shingle style
1893

Corydon T. Purdy House ⑦⑥ (not illustrated)   Normand Patton and Reynolds Fisher were prolific in their designs of Queen Anne homes in Oak Park. In this house they diverged a bit from their norm, designing in the Shingle style, which incorporated elements from the contemporaneous Queen Anne style. While this style initially appeared in coastal New England in the 1880s, Frank Lloyd Wright's first employer, Joseph Lyman Silsbee, popularized the form in the Midwest, and Wright's own Oak Park home ① is a Shingle-style cottage. This house features many exuberant elements, from the wide wraparound porch, Palladian windows, oriel (or bay) window, and eyebrow dormer, to the combination of shingles and clapboard that complements the whole. The interior has four fireplaces and woodwork of pine and oak. The original owner, Corydon Purdy, a structural engineer, specialized in the use of steel construction in Chicago's early skyscrapers. A consulting engineer for the architecture firm of Holabird and Roche, he collaborated on many prominent buildings, including the landmark Marquette Building in Chicago's Loop.

76

502, 506,
510, 514,
518, 522
North Grove

Henry G.
Fiddelke
(attributed)

Tudor
Revival

1910

77

Hales Speculation Houses 77   In contrast to the sumptuous high-style Tudor Revival mansion of Burton Hales 78 , these six homes attributed to the same architect display only a few simplified elements of the Tudor Revival style, such as the high-pitched roofs and brackets beneath the eaves. They are essentially vernacular architecture which, strictly defined, signifies a structure built by a contractor rather than one designed by an architect. However, the term can also refer to inexpensive housing that reflects local building styles and materials rather than a single identifiable architectural style. Built on speculation for Hales, each home was to cost $7,000, a modest sum compared to Hales's own $45,000 home. Each pair of houses shares a common driveway leading to a two-car garage, and as originally built, they were similar in appearance. Modifications over the years – note the hipped roof at 518 North Grove and the differing wall claddings – testify to the changing needs and tastes of the owners. Architect Henry Fiddelke practiced in Oak Park for nearly forty years and designed competently in a variety of styles for diverse clients (see also 74 and 92).

Burton F. Hales House  In 1905 Mr. Hales's dream house – containing twenty-one rooms, thirteen bedrooms, and five fireplaces in its 9,500 square feet of living space – was completed on 1.3 acres at a cost of $45,000. Befitting this imposing scale, architect Henry Fiddelke chose the Tudor Revival style with its associations of grand medieval manor houses. The yellow-faced brick with Bedford limestone trim is accented by the red tile roof and the rich patina of the copper gutters, downspouts, and dormers. The Tudor Revival style is lavishly expressed in the large elaborated chimneys, crenelated parapet above the porch, stone finials terminating the wall gables, and Tudor arches. Enclosing the irregular property line, the wrought-iron fence with stone posts is a later addition. The house, porte cochere, and four-car garage are sited on the north side of the lot, allowing for gardens and a small open porch at the southern exposure. Burton Hales, a member of the firm Hales and Hunter, was on the Board of Trade for forty years.

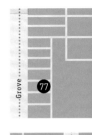

78

509 North
Oak Park

Henry G.
Fiddelke

Tudor
Revival

1904–05

Walter Hill House 79   Architect Harvey Page built the Hill House the year following his Page House on Euclid 35 . Both homes are excellent examples of the Neoclassical style, which became popular following the 1893 World's Columbian Exposition in Chicago. Called Daniel Burnham's "White City," the buildings constructed for the Exposition were classically inspired, despite rival architect Louis Sullivan's opposition. Classically influenced structures dominated public and commercial buildings for the next fifty years and were very popular in the affluent residential market. The style is defined by the monumental, full-height entry porch (which distinguishes it from Colonial Revival examples that are also classically inspired). In the Hill House the two-story porch spans almost the entire width of the facade, and four colossal Ionic columns support a pediment with a fanlight. The grand scale of the building, the symmetry of the design, and the refined, elegant proportions make this house an archetype of the Neoclassical style. Walter Hill, the owner, was the advertising manager for the Northwestern Yeast Company.

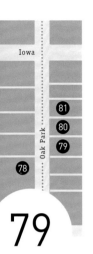

**516 North
Oak Park**

**Harvey L.
Page**

Neoclassical

1897

520 North
Oak Park

Theodore V.
Wadskier

Stick style

c. 1888

80

William M. Luff House ⑧⓪   Pretending not to be Stick style, this house
with its unrestrained facade is an exercise in texture and form. Popularized
through pattern books of the 1860s and 1870s, the Stick style grew out of
the Picturesque Gothic Revival style promoted by Andrew Jackson Downing
(see ㉘). The style takes its name from the stickwork, both applied and
structural, that was intended to reflect the truthfulness of materials. Unlike
the Gothic Revival style, which placed emphasis on ornamenting windows
and doors, in the Stick style the wall surface itself is elaborately decorated,
exemplified here in the shingles, clapboards, and stickwork. The building's
vertical lines are expressed in the cornerboards and continuous two-story
porch posts. Picturesque touches are found in the heavy wood brackets
supporting the second- and third-floor balconies, which add a Swiss Chalet
flavor, and in the jerkinhead roof that caps the two-story porch. The unusual
placement of the wraparound porch on the north facade instead of the
sunny south remains a mystery. William Luff was an attorney who practiced
in Chicago.

Charles E. Cessna House 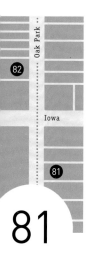   In this design E. E. Roberts presented a contrast between elements that create a feeling of heaviness and those that convey lightness. The low, wide porch roof makes the entry appear almost cavernous, darkening the entire approach to the doorway. This environment is heightened by the porch's solid brick piers with heavy scalloped wood brackets, the dark brown brick with deeply raked joints, and by the disturbingly low, hooded dormers that let in very little light. In comparison, the stucco second story with wood banding has a lighter appearance. The simple art-glass designs in the second-floor fenestration, and the windows with thin, delicate mullions that wrap around the corners (a feature Roberts also used in his mature designs), reinforce this light, airy feeling. Additional complexity is added by the two-story bay on the south facade, polygonal on the first floor and rectilinear above. Although similar in basic form to other of Roberts's designs from this period, this home has a distinctly rich appearance created through this interplay of elements. The Oak Park Directory lists Charles Cessna's business as loans.

**524 North
Oak Park**

**E. E.
Roberts**

Prairie style

1905

611 North
Oak Park

Worthmann
and
Steinbach

Chateauesque

1904

82

William Thoms House 82   Newspapers have described this two-and-a-half-story house as a miniature French Renaissance Chateau with Queen Anne features, as well as an urban Queen Anne with classic features, illustrating the difficulty of defining the exact style of a home. However, the Chateauesque elements – the masonry construction, steeply pitched hipped roof, and turret – would seem to prevail. Features that capture the eye include the assortment of window shapes – squared, Roman arched, variation on Palladian, and porthole (many with beveled and art glass) – and the variety of lintels that top the windows. Originally the exterior was even more elaborate, with copper gutters, a bracketed cornice, and a slate roof with terracotta ridge tiles. It is a delight to see the cone-shaped south bay terminated by a finial, since many pinnacles in Oak Park have been struck by lightning, and homeowners are reluctant to replace them. Inside, there are plaster ceiling medallions, oak details, multiple staircases, and pocket doors, signs of a well-appointed interior. The house was built at a cost of $12,000 for William Thoms, who, with his brothers, owned a paper company in Chicago.

Harold H. Rockwell House  83   An extra-wide watertable (the projecting ledge above the foundation that deflects rain or snow) joins this house firmly with the earth and acts as the base for the double set of piers moving from foundation to gable. In this design the piers are hollow and function as ducts through which air circulates between the attic and cellar, making the house more comfortable in the summer. Horizontal wood banding at the first-floor level and at the eaves line is the only contrast to the substantial stucco facade, a departure from the firm's usual use of wood to separate the stories. A large picture window is prominently featured on the first floor, while casement windows are used in other areas. The casement window was a favorite of the Prairie School architects because the entire window opened outward, inviting a greater connection with the outdoors. The side entrance midway along the drive lessens the sounds and distractions of a busy street. Rockwell, the owner, was a vice president at the Northern Trust Company and an Oak Park trustee.

83

629 North Oak Park

Tallmadge and Watson

Prairie style

1910

710 West Augusta

Frank Lloyd Wright

Prairie style

1913

Harry S. Adams House 84   An elegant display of Wright's mature Prairie idiom, this house is the last designed by the architect in Oak Park. The wide lot enabled Wright to emphasize the horizontal lines of the structure, one of the major themes of his career in Oak Park. A limestone beltcourse, visually separating the first and second stories, enhances this horizontal emphasis, as do the terrace and window planters that become extensions of the house. A wide rectangular chimney caps the master's work. The owner specified that the plans be drawn to take advantage of the view south toward Euclid Avenue. Wright thus arranged the porte cochere, open porch (now enclosed), living room, foyer, and dining room along this principal axis, exposing the rooms to the sun from morning until twilight. As the sun moves across this facade, the iridescent art glass in the entry door changes color. With the broad overhanging eaves, however, he ensured that the sun's rays were restrained in summer and allowed in during winter. Inside the wood trim along the ceilings defines a continuous flow of space from one room to another. Some of the original fixtures, hardware, and built-in bookcases, as well as a china cabinet, remain. Though recessed, the entry is not as hidden as in Wright's earlier work, and the geometric design of the concrete urn is a welcoming symbol at the steps. The original property line extended east almost to the corner of Augusta and Linden. The office of Dr. Adams, a surgeon, was located in downtown Chicago.

84

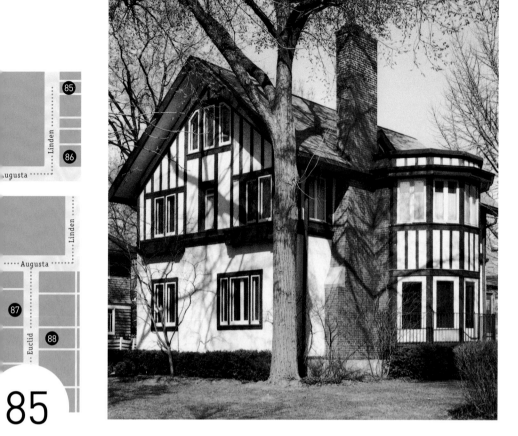

730 North Linden

Tallmadge and Watson

Prairie style

1915

John W. Bingham House 85   With over 250 buildings in the Chicago area credited to Tallmadge and Watson, we are fortunate to have a varied representation in Oak Park. Built at the end of the Prairie period, this modest-sized house is one of the last structures with Prairie features built by the firm in the village. While the facade's half-timbering evokes the Tudor Revival style and in part portends the firm's later preference for revival styles, it is also a device common in Prairie architecture. Here it is used, together with the beltcourse that divides the first and second stories, to create a dynamic interplay between the horizontal and the vertical lines of the facade. In the interior spaces the birch banding continues the dialogue between the vertical and horizontal and unifies the individual areas in a typical Prairie manner. The interesting window placement is a notable departure from the light screens (continuous bands of windows) predominant in Prairie architecture. Bingham, the owner, was a general agent for the Indiana Harbor Belt Railway.

William H. Gardner House 86 (not illustrated)   A three-story, poured-concrete residence, this home was built for the sum of $10,000. The rectilinear design – a straightforward, non-historical style common in Oak Park between 1900 and 1915 and popularized by E. E. Roberts – features minimal woodwork, a gabled roofline, and prominent dormers, starting a trend away from the Prairie style. However, the Prairie influence can still be seen in the wide overhanging eaves, the grouped windows on the first floor, and the relatively open interior plan. The curved arch over the entry, repeated in the windows on the same facade, is a gracenote in this otherwise simple house. Later additions of an informal dining room and rear studio were done in the 1980s with respect to the original design. At this time shutters were added, as well as a beautiful Japanese garden. William Gardner, the owner, was in the lumber business in Chicago. Edgar Rice Burroughs, the creator of Tarzan, lived here for a short time prior to moving to California in 1918 to supervise the filming of his stories.

700 North Linden

E. E. Roberts

Prairie style

1911

86

George C. Page House 87   Called "one of the grand dames of the village," this romantic early Neoclassical home, aptly named "Whitewood," exemplifies the influence of the classically inspired buildings of the 1893 World's Columbian Exposition. The original central portion of the two-story porch, with columns supporting a classical pediment, points directly to the fair's Virginia pavilion – a copy of Mount Vernon, one of the first houses in the country to have a porch extending to the top of the facade. Other details informed by the classical revival include the symmetry of the house, the Palladian windows, the doorway crowned by a fanlight, the row of dentils under the eaves, and the fanlight repeated in the triangular pediment. The interior is laid out in traditional fashion, with rooms radiating from the central foyer. The sweeping full-width porch with triple columns at the corners, the two-story projecting south bay, and enlarged kitchen were 1905 alterations and harmonize well with the original design. Attorney George Page, the first owner, lived in the house less than ten years. His brother, Harvey Page, an architect prominent in Washington, D.C., designed the house.

637 North Euclid

Harvey L. Page

Neoclassical

1896

87

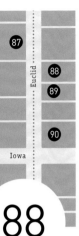

Ashley C. Smith House 88 In this stately house standing prominently on an ample lot, Tallmadge and Watson applied a mixture of Prairie elements to a simple rectilinear base. The large, sheltering one-story porch is an unusual feature in the Oak Park work of Tallmadge and Watson, and the trademark piers that the architects used in most of their homes (see 33) are barely visible flanking the entry. Similar designs can be seen in the architects' work in Chicago's north shore suburbs. The house also shares elements with other Oak Park homes of the period: the contrasting stucco and red brick; the art glass in the main doorway (repeated in the second- and third-floor windows above); and the hipped roof (originally covered with tiles). The curved dormer on the main facade, the shape of which is echoed in the windows of the study above the porte-cochere, is another feature found in other Prairie houses. The owner, Ashley Smith, a banker, was only able to enjoy his wonderful house for a short time before he died.

**630 North
Euclid**

**Tallmadge
and Watson**

**Prairie style
1908**

620 North
Euclid

E. E.
Roberts

Tudor
Revival

1904

Henry C. Todd House 89   E. E. Roberts, an architect who designed in a
number of styles, chose to focus on baronial Tudor forms to engage this massive lot. The finished house, with fourteen rooms and fourteen-inch-thick
walls, presided over grounds with a 125-foot frontage on Euclid, extending
back 350 feet, and a 100-foot frontage on Linden. The Tudor influence is
seen in the half-timbering and the immense gables with heavy supporting
brackets, as well as in the seventy-seven leaded-glass windows of diamond
shapes and tulip patterns. The combination of brick and stucco, common in
Tudor Revival houses throughout America, was particularly popular in Oak
Park and was used in houses of many types, as were red tile roofs. Though
some of the property on Linden has since been sold, the house remains a re-
gal, impressive structure. The village building permit lists the cost as
$10,000, a reasonable amount for a house and lot of these proportions.
Henry Todd was president of the Chicago Fireproof Covering Company.

89

d

George D. Webb House  Featured in a 1913 publication *Country and Suburban Homes of the Prairie School Period*, this house was referred to as "an attractive country residence combining elegance with good taste." The rectilinear brick house for a partner in the insurance firm of Conkling, Price and Webb is representative of the variations of Prairie School designs built during the style's greatest popularity. The hipped roof (originally covered in clay tile) and the wood beltcourse – separating the brick of the first floor from the cream-colored stucco of the second floor – are typical elements of the Prairie style. These indicative features are softened by other functional and aesthetic elements that made the house suitable for a conservative client. At the main entry stairs on Iowa Street, flower urns filled with seasonal blooms make a welcoming statement; screened porches on the west facade of both the first and second floors took advantage of summer breezes at a time before central air conditioning; and the original landscaping created a total environment that included the covered walkway to the garage, which housed the chauffeur's quarters above.

90

600 North
Euclid

Henry K.
Holsman

Prairie style
1910

530 North
Euclid

George W.
Maher

Prairie style

1905

91

Charles R. Erwin House ⑨ By using the water lily as the main theme in this house, George Maher implemented his famous "motif rhythm" design theory – which advocated the unification of interior and exterior space by repeating two or three design elements. Unfortunately, the house and grounds have undergone major alterations, with little remaining of the architect's details save for the original delicate design of the art glass above the entry and the decorative grillwork on the basement windows. The segmental arch over the entry, garage doors, and side door was another favorite motif of the architect, as were the wide overhanging eaves that give a sense of shelter to the whole. The windows, however, grouped in twos and threes with no definite placement pattern, are an unusual choice for this architect much concerned with the formal appearance of his designs. A small open porch is a reminder of the importance placed on fresh air at this time. The building permit gives the cost of this house as $18,000. Charles Erwin, the owner, was a pioneer in the advertising field and his wife, Rachel, was a published poet.

507 North
Euclid

Henry G.
Fiddelke

Neoclassical

1903

E. P. Jennings House ⓷ (not illustrated)   Despite the fact that the modernist Prairie style was at the height of its popularity during this period, many architects continued to work in traditional forms based on historical precedent. In the Jennings House the Neoclassical style was used by architect Henry Fiddelke to create an imposing, aristocratic residence featuring the characteristic two-story porch with four pillars. It is difficult to appreciate the building's symmetry now that a small brick house sits where the original curved drive led to the main entrance. A glance across the street to 506 North Euclid shows that a similar fate befell Tallmadge and Watson's Basse House (1920) when the graceful winding driveway was replaced by a ranch house. Oak Park, a small area of 4.2 square miles, was out of vacant building space in the 1940s, when economics created pressure to subdivide properties such as these. E. P. Jennings, the owner, is listed in the Oak Park directory as a mining expert.

609 North
Linden

White and
Weber

Tudor
Revival

1928

Telfer MacArthur House ⓷   Land in this area north of Chicago Avenue was developed after World War I. At this time a wave of nostalgia prompted many architects to turn to revival styles for inspiration. This brick-veneer and stucco residence is typical of the romantic Tudor Revival style, particularly in its steep roof with overlapping gables, which form a protected entrance. A paean to English medieval times, this style is more representative of the Elizabethan age than the earlier Tudor period for which it is named. Other Tudor Revival elements include the elaborate chimney, the Lannon stone (a local limestone) quoins at the northeast corner of the building, and the Tudor-arched entrance. An eclectic touch can be seen in the small two-story pulpit bay with a copper roof. Slate, used on the main roof, was a popular roofing material in the 1920s. The original owner, Telfer MacArthur, was an early publisher of *Oak Leaves*, the major local newspaper.

Telfer MacArthur House

Euclid

91

92

Linden

94

93

Iowa

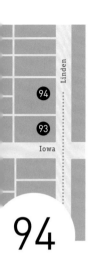

94

605 North
Linden

Charles E.
White

Prairie style

1908

James F. Skinner House  One of White's larger commissions in Oak Park, this home departs from the architect's earlier, rather simple, stucco Prairie houses. Filling a large portion of the corner lot, the structure appears bulky due to the asymmetrical massing of the porches and chimneys. A movement away from White's undivided surfaces, the decorative brick trim applied to the stucco breaks up the expanse of the facade and functions visually as a beltcourse. The low hipped roof and art-glass windows add to the Prairie style.

The building permit lists the cost of this house as $20,000, making it quite an expensive house at the time, but a fair price for the size and materials. More modest three-bedroom houses were selling for $5,000 to $6,000. The Morton Arboretum retains landscape plans for this site drawn by Jens Jensen, a well-known Chicago landscape architect dedicated to the preservation and reconstruction of native prairie lands. The owner, James Skinner, was an executive at Sears, Roebuck & Co.

tour

e

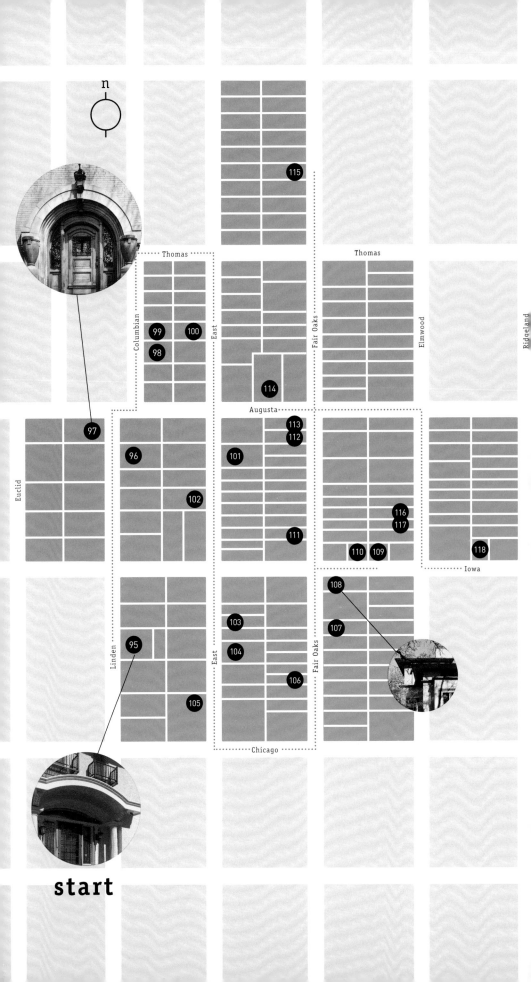

n

Thomas

Thomas

115

Columbian

East

Fair Oaks

Elmwood

Ridgeland

99   100

98

114

Augusta

97

113
112

96

101

Euclid

102

116
117

111

110   109

118

Iowa

108

Linden

103

107

95

East

104

Fair Oaks

106

105

Chicago

start

Tour E will be of special interest to individuals drawn to the pre-Prairie and transitional work of Frank Lloyd Wright, to the full spectrum of residential designs of Thomas Tallmadge and Vernon Watson, or to the various adaptations by John S. Van Bergen of Wright's 1907 *Ladies Home Journal* fireproof house project.

The five Wright residences cover the time period from 1895 to 1903, when Wright was moving into uncharted waters as his exterior and interior designs began to express respect and appreciation for the Midwestern landscape. As the freedom of the seemingly never-ending prairie inspired a simplification of Victorian vernacular designs, the Prairie vocabulary developed. Placed within the context of Wright's development, the 1895 Goodrich and the 1897 Furbeck houses (103 and 106) represent his pre-Prairie experimentation. In the 1901–02 Fricke and 1903 Martin houses (108 and 101), he moved dramatically into a more recognizable Prairie idiom, though he maintained at the heart of each design a central vertical core. The 1903 Cheney House 104 is an excellent example of Wright's success in producing an authentic Prairie design with the many characteristics that determined a truly new American style of architecture.

This tour also offers the greatest concentration of Tallmadge and Watson designs, including six attributed to Watson or the firm, and a 1905 collaboration between Watson and Lawrence Buck. Both principals participated in the stimulating, radical dialogue at the Chicago Architectural Club, a forum for emerging Prairie School archi-

tects. Tallmadge and Watson's Prairie-style designs remained distinctive, never imitating Wright or other contemporaries. Besides the houses featured in the tour, those with specific interest in Tallmadge and Watson can observe the history of the firm's responses to changes in public taste and market conditions between 1904 and 1928. Spanning this period are seven residences concentrated in the 600 block of Fair Oaks: 601 (Mather, 1928), 611 (Carroll, 1913 111), 614 (Lewes, 1928), 626 (Lauder, 1907), 636 (Kittle, 1909), 643 (Watson, 1904 112), and 645 (McFeely, 1905 113).

Finally, Oak Park native John S. Van Bergen successfully utilized Wright's 1907 fireproof project in a number of modest homes. Seven of his thirteen designs in Oak Park are included in this tour. He perfected the form in his early residences and continued to refine the basic model throughout his long career. Van Bergen worked within the Prairie idiom longer than any of his contemporaries.

Tour **E** is approximately 1.7 miles

Estimated walking time 90 minutes

530 Linden

E. E.
Roberts

Italian
Renaissance
Revival

1912

95

Mrs. S. S. Vaughn House 95   With fluted columns flanking the recessed entranceway, the symmetrical arrangement of the facade, and hipped roof originally of tile, this substantial house was strongly influenced by Italian Renaissance models. The style was part of the trend in American architecture, begun in the late-eighteenth century, that revived historical designs, exemplified in the more popular Tudor Revival and Colonial Revival styles. Although the Prairie School rejected such European dominance, E.E. Roberts, the most prolific Oak Park architect, was capable of working successfully in a variety of styles to please his clients. The Vaughn House also shows the influence of the Prairie style, which was at its height in 1912. The eye is drawn to the grace and dignity of the arched, bracketed canopy over the entry, and then upward to the central dormer that mimics the dominant canopy. The segmental arches, and their relationship to one another, recall the work of George Maher (see 48 and the Pleasant Home, a house museum in Oak Park.)

Henry D. Golbeck House 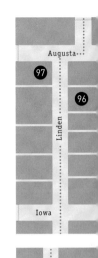 An example of the fully developed Prairie designs of Tallmadge and Watson, this L-shaped residence was built for furniture manufacturer Henry Golbeck. The house is similar to other mature designs by the firm, specifically the Carroll ⑪, Babson II ㊳ , Rockwell ㊸ , and Guy I ㊅ houses. Signature characteristics include the decorative wood trim (similar to Tudor Revival half-timbering) that follows the pitch of the west gable, the high beltcourse that separates the red brick and stucco, the casement windows sheltered by wide overhanging eaves, and the hidden side entrance. The living room, running the width of the west facade, is dominated by a Roman brick fireplace wall without a mantle, an element often used in Tallmadge and Watson designs. The interior woodwork is particularly rich – birch with narrow mahogany accent trim and quarter-sawn oak paneling in the dining room.

96

636 Linden
Tallmadge
and Watson
Prairie style
1914–15

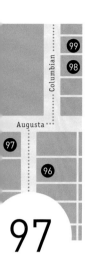

97

647 Linden

Frederick R.
Schock

Italian
Renaissance
Revival

1924

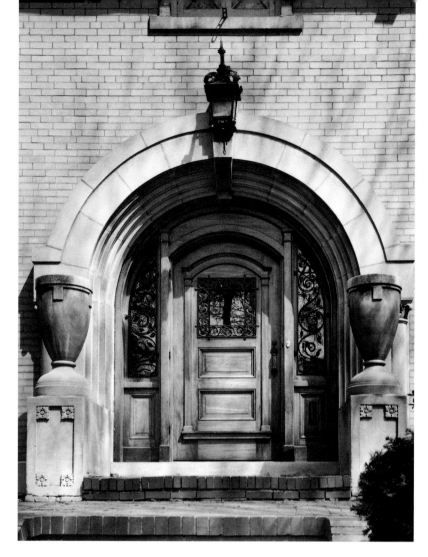

C. S. Castle House 97   Most of Frederick Schock's work was in Austin, the Chicago community to the east of Oak Park, where both Schock and Castle family members were officers of the Austin State Bank. The Castle House, completed ten years before Schock's death, is very different from his early, shingled, turn-of-the-century Queen Anne residences, which were often quite complex and dramatic (as in his own 1886 Austin home at 5804 Midway Park). In the Castle House Schock used the Italian Renaissance Revival style (see also 95) to create a substantial and conservative facade. In the post–World War I period when it was constructed, historical revival styles were in vogue. Corresponding with the decline in popularity of the Prairie style, the appeal of these styles was fueled by a nostalgic interest in all things historical, as well as by improved masonry veneering techniques that allowed closer imitations of the original Italian structures. The tower, replete with crenelated parapet, raises speculation about Schock's sense of humor when he created this castle-like dwelling for the Castle family.

Robert N. Erskine House 98 (not illustrated)   The Erskine House, its neighbor the Griess House 99 , and the Barlow House 100 are significant because each is a Van Bergen variation of the famous fireproof Prairie-house project by Frank Lloyd Wright. After Wright had successfully designed Unity Temple in 1905 using newly developed poured concrete, he was commissioned by the Curtis Publishing Company to produce a low-cost residential Prairie design using the same technology. Wright's solution, a $5,000 fireproof house, was published with a description and construction details in the April 1907 issue of *Ladies Home Journal*. Two years after publication of the design, Van Bergen was hired by Wright and was the last associate to work with him in the Oak Park studio. Many of Van Bergen's residential designs of modest cube-shaped homes drew from Wright's concept, three of them as noted above, as well as four additional variations, Mrs. Charles S. Yerkes 109 , Harry Horder 115 , Albert Manson 116 , and Mrs. R. D. Manson 117 houses. In total, there are thirteen Van Bergen "cube" houses in Oak Park.

Philip Griess House 99 (not illustrated)   The Griess and Erskine 98 houses are two versions of Van Bergen's cube houses. In these houses, his basic formula consists of a two-story square topped with a hipped or flat roof. Most often a central chimney is located within the main mass, and a one-story porch (normally enclosed) is positioned for the best light; the entry, not visible from the street, usually is located on the side of the house opposite the porch. (The Erskine House partially contradicts the formula since the entry and the open porch are together on the south facade.) Prairie characteristics include banded casement windows and exterior wood trim emphasizing the geometric proportions of the main massing. An unusual feature here is the studio located on the second floor above the entry; a similar studio is incorporated into the design of the Mrs. Charles S. Yerkes House 109 .

714
Columbian
John S. Van
Bergen
Prairie style
1913

98

716
Columbian
John S. Van
Bergen
Prairie style
1914

99

717 North
East Ave.

John S. Van
Bergen

Prairie style

1923

100

John Barlow House 100 (not illustrated)   The John Barlow House is the third of three (see 98 and 99) Van Bergen permutations of small cube houses in this section of the tour. A more expensive version, this house is finely articulated with a high brick beltcourse and subtle variations in the brickwork. Following Van Bergen's typical formula, an enclosed sunroom is attached on the south side. One departure from his usual design, however, is the front entry that is visible and accessible directly from the street. A small, functional hidden balcony adds interest above the entry. The Barlow House was commissioned following World War I after Van Bergen had moved to Highland Park, Illinois, where he maintained an independent practice. His designs retained the Prairie vocabulary until the 1950's. Upon relocating to California in 1955, Van Bergen's late work reflected the modern architecture of the period.

636 North
East Ave.

Frank Lloyd
Wright

Prairie style

1903

101

William E. Martin House 101   In 1903 Wright was still experimenting with the convergence of strong vertical elements and powerful horizontal lines. After the completion of the William Martin House, however, Wright moved away from dominant vertical elements in his designs. As with its sister, the Fricke House 108 , here the eye feasts on the intersections of planes and elements: stucco with wood, tiered roof overhangs with hidden porches, and the interior space opening to the exterior. The horizontal lines are emphasized by banded geometric windows, continuous sills, and the recently reconstructed front garden wall, which originally extended across the lot to the south and enclosed a large garden with pergola and pools. Wright received several commissions as a result of the William Martin House, including the famous 1903 Larkin Company Administration Building and the 1904 Darwin Martin House in Buffalo, New York. Darwin Martin, an officer in the Larkin Company, was the brother of William Martin.

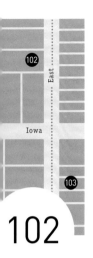

Barrett Andrews House 102   Vernon Watson, an Oak Park resident, and Thomas Tallmadge, from Evanston, formed a partnership in 1905. Very likely this early commission was Watson's work. The Midwest craftsman cottage draws inspiration from the English Arts and Crafts movement, much like the 1905 Reeves House 110, which was a collaboration between Watson and Lawrence Buck. The building stands on a double lot that encouraged a broad, expansive design. This horizontal character is emphasized by the forty-five-foot-wide porch, hipped roofs, narrow dark brown clapboard siding, and grouped casement windows. The high, slightly flared poured concrete foundation was often used in the firm's early designs. The open interior is created by the uninterrupted flow between the living room, entry hall, and dining room; just a suggestion of dermarcation is given by rectilinear posts. Oak trim is accented by exceptional hammered copper Arts and Crafts sconces in the shape of the Tree of Life. In 1996 a meticulous restoration and an historically sensitive addition were completed, doubling the size of the original house. The present owners have carefully landscaped the grounds with turn-of-the-century period gardens.

623 North
East Ave.

Tallmadge
and Watson

Prairie style

1906

534 North
East Ave.

Frank Lloyd
Wright

pre-Prairie

1895–96

Harry C. Goodrich House 103   Wright's experimentation in the mid-
1890s is evident in the home he designed for inventor Harry Goodrich. Here
he simplified the typical picturesque, complex massing of the Victorian
styles, giving a geometric purity to the design. Two visually significant elements in the Goodrich House relate to the 1897 Rollin Furbeck House 106,
which shares an alley with the Goodrich residence: the great pagoda-like
roof (a Japanese influence) that crowns the rectangular mass, and the two-
story front bay emphasizing the vertical center of the house. Wright
introduced horizontal elements through the narrow clapboard siding that
rises to the sill line of the second-floor windows, the exceptionally wide
projecting eaves, and the stucco band linking the upper windows. The geometric casement windows in the central bay also point to Wright's later
preferences. As in the Furbeck House, the screened front porch appears as
a miniature of the main structure, converging with it at a right angle to
form a hidden entrance.

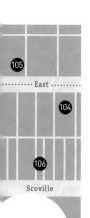

East

105

104

106

Scoville

104

520 North
East Ave.

Frank Lloyd
Wright

Prairie style

1903–04

Edwin H. Cheney House 104   In the minds of many, the Cheney house, along with the 1902 Arthur Heurtley House 25 , marks the apex of Wright's residential work in Oak Park. While there are striking differences between the two, particularly in the settings and building materials, both represent Wright's growing mastery of the Prairie idiom. As in the Heurtley House, the massive hipped roof of the Cheney House gives shelter to the living room, dining room, and library, all of which are located on the raised main floor. The open interior spaces are integrated by a ceiling with complex wood beaming in a chevron design. More than in any other local example, the interior and exterior spaces of the Cheney residence flow seamlessly into one another. The home is of interest for more than its architecture, since it is notable for the intrigue surrounding the scandalous love affair between Wright and the client's wife, independent-minded Mamah Cheney. The clandestine liaison became public when, in 1909, Wright and Mrs. Cheney abruptly traveled to Germany, where Wright worked on the Wasmuth portfolio. The tragic ending of their relationship came in 1914, when Mrs. Cheney and her two children died in a fire at Taliesin.

M. A. Richardson/Percy Julian House 105 (not illustrated) One of the most historically significant residences in Oak Park is the home of the internationally known chemist Percy Julian (1899–1975). Among the notable achievements of Dr. Julian are his development of a treatment for glaucoma and his discovery of the synthesis for cortisone. The Alabama-born, Harvard-educated African-American broke the color barrier in Oak Park when he and his family moved into their home in 1951. Despite some strong initial opposition, the family received considerable support from neighbors. The public response to attacks on the Julians created open debate and growing support for fair housing laws, eventually resulting in the passage of the Oak Park Fair Housing Ordinance in 1968. His 1908 home, built for tinware manufacturer M. A. Richardson, is one of the few symmetrical "V"-shaped residences in Oak Park. Some of the original Prairie elements have been obscured by subsequent alterations. This substantial home, built for $15,000, was designed by Thornton Herr, a little-known Oak Park architect, who was in practice in 1907 with William G. Barfield of Chicago.

515 North East Ave.

Thornton A. Herr

Prairie style

1908

105

Rollin Furbeck House 106 Built as a wedding gift by stockbroker Warren Furbeck for his son, the Rollin Furbeck House demonstrates Wright's experimentation that would lead to the first purely Prairie design. Each level is capped by a hipped roof with wide overhanging eaves, where what appear to be classical dentils are tucked away. The open front porch, mimicking the main structure, leads to a hidden entrance; and the building's surface is divided by brick and stucco. Wright, however, was still working with vertical elements in 1897, evident in the emphasis he placed on the three-story, yellow brick core that projects beyond the main section of the house. The complex central tower has corbeled brickwork, angled piers, and octagonal columns topped with Sullivanesque organic stylized capitals. The fenestration is varied, ranging from the unadorned front plate glass window to double-hung windows to the small casement windows with fixed transoms. Many have diamond panes, which Wright used to enhance privacy and to make interior window treatments unnecessary.

515 Fair Oaks

Frank Lloyd Wright

pre-Prairie style

1897

106

Rollin Furbeck House

Rollin Furbeck House

107

106

Fair Oaks

Chicago

106

532 Fair
Oaks

Architect
unknown

1893–94

Stick style

Perkins and
Will

Colonial
Revival
remodeling
1940

107

Ella and William F. Van Bergen House (107)   The history of this house has been debated; however, recent documentation links it to the family of Prairie architect John S. Van Bergen, whose parents were prominent Oak Park citizens. The senior Van Bergen was the chief auditor of the Chicago & NorthWestern Railroad. He and his wife, whose name appears on the title record, raised their family in this house. Records indicate that the house was first remodeled in the 1920s. A second remodeling in the 1940s, by the Chicago firm Perkins and Will, left little of the original style. Early pictures depict a clapboard Stick-style residence with a wide front porch and above the main entrance, an unusual, highly decorative second-story porch. Young Van Bergen's early studio was located in the attic, where there remains an art-glass door and window, as well as plaster walls with original color and sand finish. It is interesting to speculate how much the budding architect was influenced by the construction of Wright's Fricke House (108), which he could observe from his bedroom window.

540 Fair
Oaks
Frank Lloyd
Wright
pre-Prairie
1901–02

108

William G. Fricke House 108   Of Wright's three-story Prairie structures, the Fricke House is considered by many to be the most successful. The all-stucco design, published in the 1910 Wasmuth portfolio, helped establish Wright's worldwide reputation. Its forty-five-foot central vertical mass is intersected by a complex rhythm of strong horizontal elements, all of which combine to create an artistic whole that exemplifies Wright's aesthetic genius. While there is a vertical core, the overall feel is horizontal, accentuated by the hipped roof system, wide overhangs with built-in copper gutters, bold projecting beltcourses, and bands of art-glass casement windows. Noteworthy features on the north facade are the triangular bay and two-story bank of art glass indicating the position of the interior stairwell. An entrance hidden to the side, characteristic of the Prairie style, is discovered by way of the wide, inviting steps from the street level. An original garden connected to the house by a pergola was situated to the south where a small residence now stands.

Mrs. Charles S. Yerkes House  The young Van Bergen based this modest home on his cube design derived from Wright's fireproof house project (see 98). He built the house for the widow of Charles Yerkes, a well-known Oak Park resident, and for their daughter, Mary Agnes, an accomplished local artist for whom the studio above the entrance was built. To control costs, he used wide clapboards rather than the more expensive board-and-batten siding commonly used by Wright and other architects. The chimney dominates the central rectilinear structure and indicates the importance of the fireplace, a symbol of domesticity and the main gathering point within a Prairie interior. A two-story wing on the west and an enclosed porch on the east abut the main body of the house, following Van Bergen's formula. The wide eaves of the hipped roofs and the band of casement windows with simple muntins are other hallmarks of the Prairie style.

109

450 Iowa
John S. Van Bergen
Prairie style
1912

Charles Reeves House 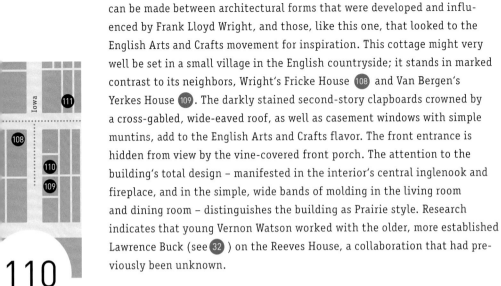 Within the Prairie style a clear distinction can be made between architectural forms that were developed and influenced by Frank Lloyd Wright, and those, like this one, that looked to the English Arts and Crafts movement for inspiration. This cottage might very well be set in a small village in the English countryside; it stands in marked contrast to its neighbors, Wright's Fricke House 108 and Van Bergen's Yerkes House 109. The darkly stained second-story clapboards crowned by a cross-gabled, wide-eaved roof, as well as casement windows with simple muntins, add to the English Arts and Crafts flavor. The front entrance is hidden from view by the vine-covered front porch. The attention to the building's total design – manifested in the interior's central inglenook and fireplace, and in the simple, wide bands of molding in the living room and dining room – distinguishes the building as Prairie style. Research indicates that young Vernon Watson worked with the older, more established Lawrence Buck (see 32) on the Reeves House, a collaboration that had previously been unknown.

110

454 Iowa

Lawrence
Buck/Vernon
Watson

Prairie style

1905

611 Fair
Oaks

Tallmadge
and Watson

Prairie style

1913

111

William V. Carroll House (111)   This simple, quietly elegant home built
for an employee of the New York Central Railroad bears the signature elements of Tallmadge and Watson's mature Prairie designs. Throughout the
period the architects captured the horizontal emphasis of the Prairie idiom
while continuing to utilize vertical elements, as seen here in the corner piers
and gable roof. The firm's seasoned designs often featured a treatment of
Tudor Revival-inspired wood trim around second-story windows that followed
the lines of the prominent gable. The cruciform plan utilized for the Carroll
House was perfected in the 1909 Torrie S. Estabrook House (63) and subse-
quently used for their 1912–13 Gustavus Babson II (58) and 1913 Joseph S.
Guy I (65) houses. In this instance, the cruciform plan creates an undifferen-
tiated living/dining space separated only by a freestanding divider that
serves as a dining buffet. The entry, stairs, kitchen (on the north), and two-
story porches (on the south) are positioned at the intersection of the axis.
The bracketed canopy which shields the side entrance, often seen in
Tallmadge and Watson designs, is likely an influence of George Maher (see (48)).

643 Fair
Oaks

Vernon S.
Watson

Prairie style

1904

112

Vernon S. Watson House 112   In the year before he went into partnership with Thomas Tallmadge, a colleague at D. H. Burnham & Company, Vernon Watson built this modest home for his bride, Emma. The Prairie influence is clearly evident in this early example of Watson's work. (It is generally thought that Watson continued to be responsible for the firm's Prairie residential designs.) Prairie characteristics include the hipped roof with wide enclosed eaves, the dominant beltcourse, and the grouped casement windows. Watson used a variety of wall cladding to enliven the facade: horizontal board-and-batten siding at the base, clapboard in the middle, and stucco above the beltcourse. The hidden entrance is accessed from the porch, which, as early photographs indicate, opened onto a south garden. In 1919 Watson added the front polygonal bay that creates a secluded second-floor balcony.

Otto McFeely House  Vernon Watson's second house in Oak Park, after his own, was for his neighbor, journalist Otto McFeely. This understated design combines the vertical and horizontal elements Watson utilized in his more mature work. The beltcourse, located high on the facade, creates an illusion of height that is accentuated by the vertical movement of the side-gabled roof. In contrast, the continuous sills of the second-story windows, which are extended by the beltcourse, provide horizontal definition. Other subtle details include the muntins in the upper sash of the first-story windows, which echo the vertical lines of the delicate balusters on the porch. These elements are similar to ones used by Watson in later commissions both for functional and decorative purposes. The front porch with its hipped roof contrasts with that of the main structure. Watson designed a rear addition in 1913.

645 Fair Oaks

Vernon S. Watson

Prairie style

1905

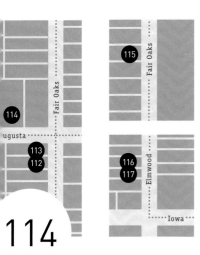

114

115

Norman S. Smith House (114) (not illustrated)   This imposing residence, with steeply pitched slate roof and prominent front chimney, is another example of the decline in the 1920s in the popularity of Prairie architecture, even in Oak Park, the birthplace of the style. In this case, the prestigious Chicago firm of Graham, Anderson, Probst and White executed a design incorporating many English Tudor expressions. The firm built many icons of downtown Chicago architecture in the 1920s and 1930s, including the Shedd Aquarium, the Wrigley Building, and Union Station. The original formal garden of the Smith House was designed by noted landscape architect Jens Jensen. A more recent owner was Joseph Randall Shapiro, a developer and attorney who founded Chicago's Museum of Contemporary Art (MCA). Shapiro's world-class art collection, including important paintings by such masters as Marc Chagall, Max Ernst, and Paul Klee, was housed in his home. Many pieces are now in the collections of the MCA, The Art Institute of Chicago, and several universities.

Harry G. Horder House (115) (not illustrated)   The home built for the Chicago mail-order businessman, Harry Horder, whose advertising asked purchasers to "Order from Horder" moves away from the simple cube designs of many modest homes by Van Bergen. Here the structure is topped with a cross-gabled roof featuring prow-angled gables, which are visually more complex than the flat or hipped roofs common to his designs. The projecting front porch, again with a gabled roof, is also uncharacteristic of the architect's early residences. The facade is quite plain, with no hint of geometric banding commonly used by Van Bergen; it is only punctuated with simply defined banks of windows.

Albert H. Manson House and Elizabeth (Mrs. R. D.) Manson House

116, **117**   Upon passing the Illinois architectural licensing examination in 1911, Van Bergen left the employ of William Drummond to establish his own practice in Oak Park. The Manson commissions, built as rental houses, are his first known independent works. Like the paired Erskine and Griess commissions (**98** and **99**), the Manson houses can easily be compared and contrasted. Both incorporate the Prairie principles of Van Bergen's cube designs, yet each varies from the other in execution of form and detail. In the Albert Manson House **116**, the mass is defined by the use of geometric trim that emphasizes the angular proportions of the cube. The wide flat roofs provide further cubic definition. In contrast, the Elizabeth Manson House **117** has a hipped roof, windows that move across the width of the facade, and extensions of the sunroom and hidden entrance that create a much more horizontal appearance. In each house the interior open plan is graced by a gray Roman brick fireplace that opens to both the living room and the dining room.

619 North Elmwood

John S. Van Bergen

Prairie style

1911

116

615 North Elmwood

John S. Van Bergen

Prairie style

1911

117

Albert H. Manson House

Elizabeth Manson House

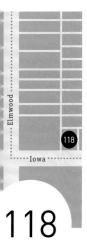

Gustavus Babson House I ⬤118 (not illustrated) The modest Babson House I is among the first known Oak Park house designed by the firm of Tallmadge and Watson after it was formed in 1905. Because Vernon Watson's social circle in Oak Park included Gustavus Babson, it is not surprising that Watson built his first house. As Watson's friend prospered, the firm ultimately designed a second, much more substantial Babson home on Linden Avenue ⬤58 in 1912–13. The first Babson House is marked by many elements that link its design to other early residences of the firm. Both the 1904 Watson ⬤112 and 1906 Andrews ⬤102 houses have hipped roofs and clapboard siding with high beltcourses, and the corner piers project through the roof of the porch to create parapets. This device is also used in the 1905 W. H. Black House, and in the porch on the side of Watson's own home ⬤112 . The standard wide, flat wood trim on the exterior and interior was characteristic of all Tallmadge and Watson designs throughout the Prairie period. The unusually beautiful art-glass front door is also notable.

118

412 Iowa

**Tallmadge
and Watson**

Prairie style

1906

Selected bibliography

Brooks, H. Allen. *The Prairie School: Frank Lloyd Wright and His Midwest Contemporaries*. Toronto: University of Toronto Press, 1975.

Carley, Rachel. *The Visual Dictionary of American Domestic Architecture*. New York: Henry Holt and Company, 1994. First Owl Book edition, 1997.

Chamberlin, Everett. *Chicago and its Suburbs*. Chicago: T. A. Hungerford & Co., 1874.

Dull, Elizabeth. "The Domestic Architecture of Oak Park, Illinois: 1900–1930." Ph.D. Dissertation, Northwestern University, 1973.

Gowans, Alan. *Styles and Types of North American Architecture: Social Function and Cultural Expression*. New York: Harper Collins Publishers, 1992.

Guarino, Jean. *Oak Park: A Pictorial History*. St. Louis: G. Bradley Publishing, Inc., 1988.

Halley, William. *Pictorial Oak Park*. Oak Park, IL: William Halley, 1898.

Hitchcock, Henry-Russell. *In the Nature of Materials: The Buildings of Frank Lloyd Wright, 1887–1941*. 5th ed. New York: Da Capo Press, 1979.

Hoagland, Gertrude. *Historical Survey of Oak Park*. Oak Park, IL: Oak Park Public Library, 1937.

LeGacy, Arthur. "Improvers and Preservers: A History of Oak Park, Illinois, 1833–1940." Ph.D. Dissertation, University of Chicago, 1967.

Manson, Grant Carpenter. *Frank Lloyd Wright to 1910: The First Golden Age*. New York: Van Nostrand Reinhold, 1958.

Massey, James and Shirley Maxwell. *Arts & Crafts*. New York: Abbeville Press, 1995.

McAlester, Virginia and Lee. *A Field Guide to American Houses*. New York: Alfred A. Knopf, 1984.

Phillips, Steven J. *Old-House Dictionary: An Illustrated Guide to American Domestic Architecture, 1600 to 1940*. Washington, D.C.: Preservation Press, 1992.

Sanderson, Arlene. *Ridgeland Revealed*. Oak Park, IL: Village of Oak Park, 1993.

Steiner, Frances. "E. E. Roberts: Popularizing the Prairie School." *The Prairie School Review*, Second Quarter, 1973, pp. 5–24.

Storrer, William Allin. *The Frank Lloyd Wright Companion*. Chicago: University of Chicago Press, 1993.

Wright, Frank Lloyd. *Studies and Executed Buildings by Frank Lloyd Wright*. New York: Rizzoli, 1986. (Reprint of the portfolio edition of 100 lithographs published in 1910 by Verlag Ernst Wasmuth A.G., Berlin.)

Other resources used were reverse directories of Oak Park, 1904–1920, and articles from local newspapers: *Oak Leaves*, 1902–present, and *Oak Park Reporter-Argus*, 1904-1906.

Style guide

Cultural trends, technological developments, and the influence of innovative architects are factors that contribute to the development of distinct architectural styles. Style classification is linked to both the period in which the structure was built and to its design. The styles listed below are, along with their periods of popularity, the major ones represented in Oak Park.

Gothic Revival, 1860s–1870s   Rare in Oak Park. Improved cutting tools made the creation of "gingerbread" wood details possible. Part of the Picturesque movement that championed the moral and aesthetic pleasures of rural living. Popularized among builders' pattern books.

a. steeply pitched, gabled roof, often with cross gables

b. gable screen with clover foil or decorative gable trim (vergeboards)

c. shaped windows, often with Gothic arch

d. windows commonly extend into gable

1

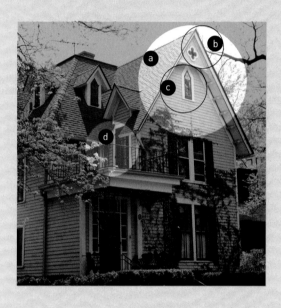

Italianate, 1860s–1880s   Popular in the Midwest but rare in Oak Park, which developed as a community after the style was in vogue. Part of the Romantic Picturesque movement that rejected the classicism of earlier styles. Many of Chicago's workers' cottages display Italianate details. Look for windows with round tops and paired brackets beneath the eaves.

a. hipped or low-pitched gable roof with wide over-hanging eaves

b. rectangular massing

c. eaves decorated with brackets, often paired

d. tall, narrow windows, often in pairs, with round tops

2

Queen Anne, 1880s–1900s   Dominated domestic architecture in the late 1800s. The exuberant ornamentation and complex shapes reflect the economic prosperity of the Gilded Age and the technology that created it. Today a careful viewer can discern the distinctive asymmetrical Queen Anne profile in houses that have lost their decorative details through later remodelings.

Shingle style, 1880s–1890s   Rare; most examples are high style. American style that evolved out of the Queen Anne style. It is less ornamented and more horizontal; distinguished by wall cladding of shingles. Popular in eastern resort towns. Exemplified by the Frank Lloyd Wright Home and Studio.

5

a. hipped or low-pitched roof with wide overhanging eaves

b. stucco or smooth-wall finish

c. banked or grouped windows

d. geometric forms and horizontal lines

Prairie style, 1900–1915   Developed as an antidote to the excesses and eclecticism of Victorian styles. Considered to be the only true indigenous American style because it did not use the "language" of preceding historic styles. Shared characteristics with English Arts and Crafts movement. Distinguished by open interior plan and integrated design of interior and exterior.

6

a. symmetrical facade

b. accentuated front door with pedimented entry porch and columns

c. multi-pane, double-hung sash windows

d. broken pediment

Colonial Revival, 1880–1955   Very common house style that has gone through different phases over the years. Interpretation of colonial styles, which often used classically derived decorative elements. Inspired by the 1876 Philadelphia Centennial. Colonial Revival details were applied to asymmetrical Queen Anne house forms in its early stages. In the 1900s more accurate interpretations of Colonial houses (generally symmetrical) were fashionable, as in the above Georgian Revival example.

Neoclassical, 1895–1950   The classically inspired architecture of the World's Columbian Exposition held in Chicago in 1893 was influential. Continued the growing interest in classical forms started with the Colonial Revival. Represented dramatic shift away from asymmetrical medieval forms popularized by the Queen Anne style. Defined by two-story, pedimented porches.

a. full-height entry porch with Ionic columns or other classical order

b. symmetrical facade with central entrance

c. elliptical, Federal-style fanlight

Tudor Revival, 1890–1940   Popular vernacular style. Interpreted medieval English architecture, ranging from simple thatched cottages to grand manor houses. Part of the historic revival movement that peaked in the 1920s and included "period" styles such as the Colonial Revival and Italian Renaissance Revival. Revival styles did not mix stylistic elements from different historic periods like the styles of the Victorian era.

a. steeply pitched roof with dominant front-facing gable

b. masonry and stucco facade, often with half-timbering

c. tall, narrow multi-pane windows

d. massive chimney

7

8

Architects' biographies

Arnold, Wesley Asbury
Watertown, N.Y., 1850–1900
After Wesley Arnold graduated from Syracuse University in 1879, he was hired in 1882 as a draftsman for the Chicago & NorthWestern Railroad. A year later Arnold married Florence Crandall, the daughter of one of Oak Park's early settlers, Miles Crandall. He concentrated on designing churches after 1885 and built more than thirty-five in the Chicago area. In addition to his own house in the Ridgeland-Oak Park Historic District (130 S. Kenilworth, 1888), Arnold built several other residences in Oak Park, including Ernest Hemingway's birth home. See entry 46.

Buck, Lawrence
New Orleans, La., 1866–1929
Prairie School
Buck was employed in Birmingham, Alabama, at the architectural firm of Sutcliffe, Armstrong, and Willett in the 1880s; and by 1894 he was working in Chicago for Sutcliffe. Between 1903 and 1905, he worked in Rockford, Illinois, where he designed eleven buildings. He then worked briefly as an architectural renderer for George Maher before opening a Chicago practice in 1906. Although he maintained his Chicago office for much of his career, Buck preferred to work out of his home studio in Ravinia, Illinois, where he also designed many residences. His work is more similar to designs by English Arts and Crafts architects – who looked to medieval cottage architecture for inspiration – than those by Frank Lloyd Wright and his followers. He was also a noted watercolorist whose work was exhibited at The Art Institute of Chicago. See entries 32, 110.

Ellis, Frank Marion
Bethany, N.Y., 1845–1933
After his discharge from the Union Army, Ellis settled in Oak Park, where he lived for the remainder of his life. Though he did not receive his formal architecture license until late in his career, in 1909, Ellis designed many important early structures in Oak Park and Austin, working as a contractor and builder. He designed in a variety of styles, including Stick style and Queen Anne. At various times he also ran manufacturing businesses, and he had a short partnership (1894-1896) with Henry Fiddelke, during which they designed sixteen homes, most of which were in Oak Park. See entry 8.

Fiddelke, Henry George
Matteson, Ill., 1865–1931
Henry Fiddelke practiced in Oak Park for nearly forty years. During his early career, he apprenticed in Chicago in the offices of Joseph L. Silsbee; Adler and Sullivan; and Jenney and Mundie. In 1894 he went into partnership with Frank Ellis in Oak Park, and two years later he opened his own office at 203 Marion Street. Despite the fact that he was a productive Oak Park architect working during the height of the Prairie School, Fiddelke did not usually work in that style, preferring historical styles instead, although some of his interiors did have Prairie attributes. Included in the guidebook is a high-style Tudor-Revival mansion, a group of modest single-family homes built by a developer on speculation, and a more formal Neoclassical house. See entries 74, 77, 78, 92.

Holsman, Henry K.
1866–1960
Henry Holsman was in partnership with W. L. Brainerd from 1893 to 1897 and served as the firm's chief designer. In 1900 he patented the "Holsman" automobile, the first two-cylinder car in this country, which was a "high wheeler" made to navigate muddy roads and ruts. He designed two buildings at the University of Chicago, as well as his wonderful metamorphosis of a university storage room into the Chapel of The Holy Grail (1930) at Disciples Divinity House. He also built the majority of buildings at Parsons College in Fairfield, Iowa. Holsman's interest and work in public and multi-family housing occupied his later career. He was also a partner in a real-estate firm in Hyde Park. See entry 90.

Maher, George Washington
Mill Creek, W. Va., 1864–1926
Prairie School
George Maher was educated in the public schools of New Albany, Indiana, and, at the age of eighteen, he began his architectural apprenticeship in the office of Bauer and Hill in Chicago. In the early 1880s he began working in the office of Joseph L. Silsbee, where he received most of his training and, in 1887, met Frank Lloyd Wright. In 1888 Maher launched his own practice designing homes in Edgewater and Kenilworth, communities that he also helped plan.

Like Louis Sullivan and Wright, he rejected traditional styles and searched for a new and indigenous American style. Maher created his own distinct version of the Prairie style – very different from Wright and his followers – which he introduced in his Oak Park masterpiece, Pleasant Home (located at 217 South Home Avenue), now a house museum National Historic Landmark. In this house and others, he applied his "motif-rhythm" theory, a system of design that involved repeating two or three decorative elements or "motifs" throughout a building to create a harmonious, unified whole. Maher's later career is marked by more derivative European-influenced designs. See entries 48, 91.

Page, Harvey L.
Washington, D.C., 1859–1934

Harvey Page began his architectural training in the office of J. L. Smithmeyer in our nation's capital. By 1886 he was an established American Institute of Architects member and had published a booklet entitled *Architectural Designs by Harvey L. Page*, a combined portfolio and promotional piece. In Oak Park his two Neoclassical designs reflect the influence of the classical buildings of Chicago's 1893 World's Columbian Exposition. He designed similar houses in Evanston and Hyde Park. Page credits H. H. Richardson – an individualistic architect whose designs laid the groundwork for the modernist style of Sullivan and Wright – as his major influence, which is more evident in the architect's East Coast work. He maintained offices in Washington and New York, but in 1895 his office is also listed in the Chicago city directory. In 1897 he went into a short-lived partnership with Lemuel Norris and Stanford Hall in Chicago. Later in his career he moved to San Antonio, Texas, where he practiced until his death. See entries 79, 87.

Patton, Normand Smith
Hartford, Conn., 1852–1915

Patton was educated in the public schools of Chicago and graduated from Amherst College with a Bachelor of Arts in 1873 and a Master of Arts in 1876; he also studied architecture in 1874 at the Massachusetts Institute of Technology. After beginning his career as a draftsman in Boston, he moved to Washington, D.C., and worked in the office of the supervising architect for the Treasury Department. In Chicago he formed with Reynolds Fisher the firm of Patton and Fisher in 1883, which was responsible for most of Patton's Oak Park residential designs. During the time he served as architect for the Chicago Board of Education (1896–1898), he went into partnership with Grant Miller to form Patton, Fisher, and Miller; by 1900 records indicate that Miller was his sole partner.

An extremely versatile architect, Patton was adept at designing a wide range of building types in a variety of styles, although he never adopted the Prairie style. He established a reputation as an architect of schools and libraries by designing such buildings as the Chicago Academy of Sciences (1893), and the Armour Institute of Technology (1891-1893) - now a part of the Illinois Institute of Technology. His efforts to awaken people to the need for public parks and green space in Chicago contributed to the establishment of a lakefront park system. He resided at 225 N. Grove in Oak Park. See entries 20, 22, 35, 51, 62, 76.

Pond, Allen Bartlit
Ann Arbor, Mich., 1858–1929

After Allen Pond received a Bachelor of Arts degree from the University of Michigan in 1880, he taught for three years at Ann Arbor High School and then at Michigan State University. Before entering architectural practice with his older brother Irving in 1886, Pond served as an assistant to his father, the warden at the State Prison in Jackson, Michigan. This exposure may have led to his interest in the field of social reform and the settlement-house movement; he was closely associated with Jane Addams of Hull House and was president of the Gads Hill Settlement. He founded the Municipal Voters League of Chicago, served on the boards of the Union League Club and the Cliff Dwellers Club, and acted as chairman of the City Zoning Board of Appeals and director of the National Housing Association. He was also a member of many committees at the American Institute of Architects and was made a fellow in 1907. See entry 49.

Pond, Irving Kane
Ann Arbor, Mich., 1857–1939

Like his younger brother Allen, Irving Pond studied at the University of Michigan; he graduated in 1879 with a degree in civil engineering. His architectural apprenticeship in the offices of Major William Le Baron Jenney and Solon Spencer Beman in Chicago was supplemented by two years of travel and study in Europe. In 1886 he formed the firm of Pond & Pond with his brother. The Pond brothers were concerned with both the social and

[Pond, Irving K., continued] aesthetic aspects of architecture. Their study of the requirements of settlement house facilities resulted in designs for Chicago Commons and Hull House, organizations with which they were closely associated

In the late 1890s Pond & Pond shared office space in Steinway Hall with a group of young architects and artists credited with the development of a new architectural movement – the Prairie School. The brothers were slightly older than most of the group and already well-established architects. Although they shared many ideas with the Prairie School, including a rejection of derivative historical styles, Irving Pond, the designer of the firm, was not a proponent of the Prairie movement. Both rejected applied ornament in favor of using the building materials themselves for decorative effect; brick was their favored medium. In 1908 Irving Pond was elected president of the American Institute of Architects. See entry 49.

Roberts, Eben Ezra
Boston, Mass., 1866–1943
Prairie School
E. E. Roberts learned freehand and mechanical drawing from his father, a woodcarver. After attending Tilton Academy in New Hampshire, he moved to Chicago. He was hired in 1889 by Solon S. Beman's firm as clerk of the works in Pullman, Illinois (now part of Chicago), the planned factory town built in the 1880s for sleeping-car magnate George Pullman. In 1893 Roberts established his own practice in Oak Park – the largest in the village's history – and designed over 200 buildings there. To achieve this output, he developed stock house types, which he varied through different decorative features – a technique also employed by Beman in his designs for Pullman. He worked well in a variety of styles, including Prairie, and catered to popular tastes, advertising him-

self as an architect of "homey dwellings." His Prairie-style designs not only demonstrate the style's increasing acceptance in Oak Park, but helped popularize the style throughout the Midwest.

Roberts also built the Second Scoville Block (in the village's commercial district; 1908), the old Municipal Building (1903), and an addition to Oak Park and River Forest High School. In 1912 he moved his office to Chicago to concentrate on commercial architecture. His son Elmer went into partnership with him from 1922 or 1923 until 1926, when Roberts went into semi-retirement. He continued to live in Oak Park until his death. See entries 7, 27, 29, 30, 33, 34, 38, 39, 40, 56, 62, 70, 71, 72, 75, 81, 86, 89, 95.

Schock, Frederick R.
Chicago, Ill., 1854–1934
Frederick Schock began his architectural career at the age of eighteen with Chicago architect Henry L. Gay. In 1880 he joined Solon S. Beman's firm and worked on the design of the model factory town of Pullman, Illinois, a planned community whose focus was the manufacture of Pullman railway cars. He moved to the Chicago suburb of Austin in 1880 and later established his own practice concentrating on residential commissions for clients in Austin, Douglas Park, Garfield Park, and Kenwood, as well as Oak Park. His early buildings were in the popular Shingle and Queen Anne styles; later designs were modified Prairie structures. See entry 97.

Spencer, Robert Clossen, Jr.
Milwaukee, Wis., 1864–1953
Prairie School
Spencer graduated in 1886 with a degree in mechanical engineering from the University of Wisconsin. After briefly studying architecture at the Massachusetts Institute of Technology, he began working in Boston at Wheelwright and Haven, and then at Shepley, Rutan, and Coolidge. By 1893 he was in Chicago working at the local office

of Shepley, Rutan, and Coolidge. Two years later he went into independent practice, opening his office first in the Schiller Building next door to Frank Lloyd Wright and then in Steinway Hall, where he shared office space with other young architects and artists, many of whom later became known as the Prairie School. From 1905 to 1923 Horace Powers was Spencer's partner; their firm, Spencer and Powers, specialized in residential architecture. Spencer's Prairie designs are characterized by an overall simplicity and frequent use of half-timbering and rectangular forms.

Spencer wrote frequently on the theory and practice of domestic architecture. His informal, illustrated articles for *House Beautiful* did much to promote Prairie School designs and ideas to a national audience, and he published the first major article about Wright's work in *Architectural Review* in 1900. He also invented hardware for casement windows and founded the Chicago Casement Hardware Company in 1906 to manufacture and distribute his designs. He eventually retired to Arizona in 1938. See entries 52, 62, 69.

Steinbach, John G.
Austria, 1878–unknown
The younger partner of the firm of Worthmann and Steinbach was born in Austria and immigrated to the United States as a child. Known for its ecclesiastical design work, the firm has to its credit more than twenty churches in Chicago, including St. Mary of the Angels. In addition, the partners also received hospital commissions such as Mother Cabrini and the old Lutheran Memorial in Chicago. See entry 82.

Tallmadge, Thomas Eddy
Washington, D.C., 1876–1940
Prairie School
Tallmadge joined the Chicago firm of D. H. Burnham and Company after graduating from the Massachusetts Institute

of Technology in 1898. Awarded the Chicago Architectural Club Traveling Fellowship in 1904, he traveled to Europe for study. Upon his return in 1905, he left Burnham's office along with his colleague Vernon Watson to form a partnership that lasted until 1936. Each partner drew on complementary strengths. Watson was a gifted designer of residential, institutional, and religious structures; Tallmadge was the public partner who excelled in church design, was knowledgeable in architectural history and restoration, and taught at the Armour Institute.

The firm is best known for designing modest suburban homes. Defining features of their Prairie-style residences include an emphasis on the horizontal and the use of natural materials and open interior plans. In later years the firm turned to historical revival styles, such as the Tudor Revival, a change that coincided with the decline in popularity of the Prairie style. In the early 1930s the firm designed many significant churches around Chicago, including First Methodist Church, Evanston; First Methodist Church, Oak Park; Grace Lutheran Church, River Forest; and First Presbyterian Church, Chicago. Tallmadge also served as a member of the Architectural Commission for the Restoration of Colonial Williamsburg. His life was tragically cut short in a train accident in 1940. See entries 31, 58, 63, 64, 65, 83, 85, 88, 96, 102, 111, 118.

Van Bergen, John Shellette
Oak Park, Ill., 1885–1969
Prairie School

A native of Oak Park, Van Bergen worked for his uncle, a builder, after graduating from Oak Park and River Forest High School. He worked as a draftsman for Walter Burley Griffin, a neighbor, for two years before enrolling in architecture classes at Chicago Technical College. In 1909 he was the last person hired in Frank Lloyd Wright's Oak Park studio, supervising unfinished projects after Wright left for Europe. A year later, while studying for the Illinois licensing exams, he worked in William

Drummond's office. After receiving his license in 1911, he began his own practice in Oak Park.

During his career Van Bergen designed many Prairie-style houses that are characterized by careful planning and simplicity. His early buildings closely mirror Wright's Prairie-style work, and his houses are often mistaken for Wright's. During World War I he served in the armed forces in Washington, D.C., and was transferred to Fort Sheridan, Illinois, where he was involved in the conversion of buildings into hospital facilities. After World War I he moved to Ravinia, Illinois, and had a successful practice on the North Shore. He moved to Santa Barbara, California, in 1955 and continued to design until his death. See entries 57, 66, 67, 68, 98, 99, 100, 109.

Van Keuren, William J.
Cincinnati, Ohio, 1853–1915

Van Keuren moved to Chicago as a young man. He resided in Oak Park for thirty years and maintained offices at 84 N. LaSalle Street in Chicago. The numerous Stick-style and Queen Anne homes he designed are spread throughout Chicago, Oak Park, River Forest, Maywood, and Austin. In the 1920s many of these residences were demolished to make room for apartment buildings. Van Keuren resided at 102 S. Clinton Street in Oak Park at the time of his death. See entry 15.

Wadskier, Theodore Vigo
St. Croix, 1827–unknown

Born on the island of St. Croix in the Danish West Indies, Wadskier trained as an architect in Copenhagen at the Royal Academy of Fine Arts. In 1850 he left Denmark and worked in Philadelphia for several years. He then moved to Chicago where he practiced for twenty years, designing many schools, churches, and business blocks. He is associated with the Gothic Revival style in Chicago and designed several major churches in the Norman and English Gothic styles, all of which were lost in the Chicago Fire of 1871: First Unitarian Society's Church of the Messiah (1866), Trinity Episcopal Church (1861), and

Atonement Church (1854). Although the fire destroyed all of Wadskier's possessions, he did resume his practice. Henry Harned was his partner and successor to the firm. See entry 80.

Watson, Vernon Spencer
Chicago, Ill., 1878–1950
Prairie School
Following studies at the Armour Institute and The Art Institute of Chicago in the late 1890s, Watson was employed by D. H. Burnham. There he met Thomas Tallmadge, who became his partner in the summer of 1905. Approximately seventy houses and institutional structures in Oak Park and River Forest are attributed to the firm. Watson, the chief designer of the partnership, developed and sustained a residential style reflecting many Prairie characteristics. He created comfortable modern homes for average Americans, thereby carrying out one of the democratic principles of the Prairie School. In the 1930s he also served as one of several designers of the Diversey Housing Project in Chicago.

Watson lived quietly with his wife, Emma Bassett Watson, in Oak Park at 643 Fair Oaks (112), the first house he designed in the village. In 1936 he retired to their summer home in Berrien Springs, Michigan, because of his wife's ill health. While in retirement he was an active resident and continued some architectural work. Because of the illnesses of both Watson and his wife, they returned to Oak Park to be with relatives; he died at West Suburban Hospital. See entries 31, 58, 63, 64, 65, 83, 85, 88, 96, 110, 111, 112, 113, 118.

White, Charles Elmer, Jr.
Lynn, Mass., 1876–1936
Prairie School
After attending the Massachusetts Institute of Technology in 1895, White worked for Swift Brothers Meat Packers designing and supervising the installation of refrigerators in vessels docked in Boston harbor. He worked for the American Gas Company in Philadelphia and street railway companies in Illinois and Ohio before joining Frank Lloyd Wright's studio in 1903. Two years later he established his own firm. From 1912 to 1922 he worked in partnership with Louis R. Christie (also identified as Charles Christie) as White & Christie, and from 1923 to 1932 with Bertram Weber as White & Weber. White & Weber's best-known commission in the village is the Oak Park Post Office (1933), built in the Art Deco style.

The modernist style White used for the small stucco houses he designed between 1905 and 1915 has been compared to similar work being done in England at the time. His later Tudor-Revival houses clearly demonstrate the influence of English cottage designs. Late in his career, between 1934 and 1937, White turned his efforts to designing superior low-cost housing for the poor and participated in several slum clearance projects on Chicago's north side. He also served as the first chairman of Oak Park's zoning board; wrote two books, *Successful Homes and How to Build Them* and *The Bungalow Book;* and contributed articles to *House Beautiful, The Ladies Home Journal*, and *Country Life in America*. See entries 47, 54, 59, 60, 61, 93, 94, 115, 116, 117.

Worthmann, Henry Soltau
Germany, 1857–1946
Worthmann immigrated to the United States as a youth and came to Chicago in 1886. He established an architectural practice the following year, and in 1903 he formed a partnership with John G. Steinbach. They practiced together for twenty-five years with offices in Englewood and on the near north side of Chicago. Worthmann resided in Oak Park only for a short period. The firm designed many churches and hospitals in Illinois, Indiana, Wisconsin, and Michigan. He lectured on the subject of church architecture in Lutheran schools and authored *The Advent of Church Architecture According to Bible History*. In 1898 he joined the Illinois Society of Architects. See entry 82.

Wright, Frank Lloyd
Richland Center, Wis.,
1867–1959
Prairie School
Frank Lloyd Wright was born in Richland Center, Wisconsin, and spent his youth on his aunts' and uncles' farm in Spring Green. He was enrolled for two semesters at the University of Wisconsin before moving to Chicago in 1887. Initially he trained with Joseph Lyman Silsbee, then moved to the offices of Adler and Sullivan, where he worked from 1888 to 1893. He established an independent practice first in the city of Chicago and then in Oak Park. His early Queen Anne and Shingle-style work evolved during his Oak Park years into simple, bold, geometric buildings. These designs, characterized by horizontal lines and broad roofs, came to be called Prairie style. While in Oak Park Wright designed more than 125 buildings and trained more than twenty apprentices in his studio. In 1909 Wright left for Europe, where he published the large and influential Wasmuth drawing portfolio. In 1911 he closed his Oak Park studio and returned to Wisconsin to build Taliesin, his new home. Later he established an architectural fellowship in Spring Green. In 1937 he designed a third home, Taliesen West, near Phoenix, Arizona. Wright's impact on Oak Park elevated the village from a center of provincial architecture to one of international acclaim. See entries 1, 2, 3, 4, 5, 6, 9, 16, 17, 18, 24, 25, 26, 36, 42, 43, 50, 53, 73, 84, 101, 103, 104, 106, 108.